Teachers
Today

To my father, Edward Zabolio,
and my grandmother, Sadie Albel,
whose lives were characterized by dignity and caring.

Teachers Today

A Guide to Surviving Creatively

Mary Zabolio McGrath

CORWIN PRESS, INC.
A Sage Publications Company
Thousand Oaks, California

For information address:

Corwin Press, Inc.
A Sage Publications Company
2455 Teller Road
Thousand Oaks, California 91320

SAGE Publications Ltd.
6 Bonhill Street
London EC2A 4PU
United Kingdom

SAGE Publications India Pvt. Ltd.
M-32 Market
Greater Kailash I
New Delhi 110 048 India

Printed in the United States of America

Library of Congress Cataloging-in-Publication Data

McGrath, Mary Zabolio.
    Teachers today : a guide to surviving creatively / Mary Zabolio McGrath.
       p. cm.
    Includes bibliographical references.
    ISBN 0-8039-6336-X (cloth). — ISBN 0-8039-6229-0 (pbk.)
    1. Teachers—United States—Job stress. 2. Burn out (Psychology)
I. Title.
LB2840.2.M35   1995
371.1'001'9—dc20   95-9037

This book is printed on acid-free paper.

95 96 97 98 99 10 9 8 7 6 5 4 3 2 1

Corwin Press Production Editor: S. Marlene Head

Contents

Preface   vii

• Why Another Book on Teacher Stress? • Who Should
Read This Book? • Description of Contents

Acknowledgments   xi

About the Author   xii

1   Living With Stress Creatively   1

• A Definition of Present-Day Educational Stress • The
Stress-Burnout Connection • Creating a Stress Profile

2   Taking Charge of Your Own Self-Care   13

• Health-Related Habits—Taking Charge of the Basics
• Health Enhancers • Enhancers to Improve Job
Function • Working It Out—Ways to Address Personal
Issues • Acting It Out—Ways to Improve Relational
Skills • Making Job-Related Changes

3   Building Bridges, Creating Cooperation   48

• Collegial Support • Creating Your Own Network
• Administrator-Administrator Support
• Administrator-Teacher Support • Teacher-
Administrator Support • Creating a Supportive
Work Environment

4 Tips for Personal Intellectual Development   75

    • Obstacles to Intellectual Growth • Ways to Grow
Intellectually • Passive Learning Opportunities
• Moving From Passive to Active Intellectual Activity
• Active Learning Opportunities • Our Best Learning
Opportunity

5 Attending to the Inner Life: Ways to Grow   91

    • Attitude • Affirmations • Self-Talk • Humor
• Keeping a Journal • Creativity • Spirituality
• Solitude

6 Creating Flexibility, Openness, and Adaptability   111

    • Flexibility • Openness • Adaptability

References   115

Preface

Today's world has fashioned a unique set of daily challenges for educators that requires them to adapt to a broad range of situations. Teachers today face circumstances in an average workday that would have been unheard of a generation ago. Cultural and economic conditions present teachers with students who arrive at school with complex problems and needs. Within this context as well are teachers seeking solutions, not only for the educational and emotional needs of students but also for their own personal survival.

Teacher stress has been a topic of popular discussion in recent times, and much research has been done to document its existence. Yet studies and data say little to those of us who experience such stress daily. What means more is an affirmation of the existence of our reality, validation as professionals, and concrete support and suggestions for handling this stress as it now presents itself.

I've researched teacher stress—jokingly, I've told people that I earned a doctorate in stress. That's true based not only on the subject of my research but also on my teaching experiences.

As a teacher of emotionally behaviorally disordered (EBD) students, I experienced burnout to the point of having to temporarily leave teaching. It was during my leave of absence and gradual recovery of my physical and emotional well-being that I developed a new and more authentic perspective on teacher stress. Looking back on my career during this pivotal time, I was able to reflect on ways I'd responded to stressful situations both as a regular and special education teacher. I took time to examine how I'd successfully coped and considered teachers who handled themselves well on the job. I then decided that once I resumed and reestablished my career, the next step would be to share with other educators workable ways in which they could not only survive creatively in their profession but thrive as well.

Why Another Book on Teacher Stress?

This is not the first book ever written on teacher stress by any means. After examining the range of other publications written on this topic in the past decade, I find many valuable resources that present well-researched discussions of teacher stress and burnout. Such books are comprehensive and discuss many dimensions of stress in sociohistorical contexts. But I question how helpful such discourse would have been to me when I was spiraling through the stress cycle heading toward burnout. In face of that, would the average teacher battling through each challenging quarter or struggling to make it from holiday to holiday take the time to dig through such material to find answers for his or her daily needs? Could such a teacher identify with an author who merely researched the topic from afar without having been there?

In contrast, this book presents clear discussions by a practicing teacher who has not only examined and compiled the data and intellectually considered the subject but who left teaching, broken and uncertain of ever regaining the psychological wherewithal to return to an educational setting again.

Although I believe I've passed through the worst job stress that my career can deal me, I still need to continue working on stress management and personal growth. Beyond that, I continue to search for ways to become a fuller, healthier, more whole individual as well.

Who Should Read This Book?

Teachers Today: A Guide to Surviving Creatively joins the stress literature primarily to provide encouragement to teachers who would like not only to handle stress at school but also to improve their general well-being. It is for those who grapple with modern teaching realities and need to maintain balance. In addition, it is written for those in administration who observe teachers in their daily struggles and wish to offer help and encouragement but aren't sure what that entails. It is for future teachers who, with this guidebook, will be better able to navigate their career paths. Finally, this book is for teacher trainers willing to provide fresh insight into the realities of teaching today for those who will teach tomorrow.

Description of Contents

In the pages ahead, you, the reader, will be able to reflect on your own occupational stress. If you are a beginner or in training for the teaching profession, you will be provided with the opportunity to consider ways you can take care of yourself as you pursue your future career. If you are an administrator or teacher trainer, you will very likely call to mind those you have known or those now in your midst who, if provided support and encouragement, would better cope and even blossom in their teaching situations.

The book begins by defining teacher stress in the context of our present society with its unique cultural influences, and it names ways that teachers experience stress both physically and behaviorally. Readers of chapter 1 will be able to focus in on their own stress symptoms and create a personal stress profile.

In the second chapter, readers will be given 30 areas of consideration for their self-care, ranging from diet to leaving the teaching profession. This chapter includes a form to help readers prioritize and take charge of their own self-care.

The third chapter examines collegial support and administrative support, both substantive means for dealing with job stress. Readers are encouraged to recognize interpersonal resources that may be readily available but have never been tapped. Support is put forth here as mutual, not only between teachers but also among administrators and their staffs. The old models of relating are challenged to encourage the creation of supportive bridges among educators in all roles.

Once readers have developed a stress management strategy, the book invites the reader to explore another means of personal growth, intellectual development. Chapter 4 gives numerous ways readers can expand their minds outside their own academic disciplines and apart from school-related pursuits.

Another stress-fighting, growth-producing area is portrayed in chapter 5, where the "inner life" is explored. Seekers who wish to examine options for growth of the inner self will find eight means to further enhance well-being.

The final chapter sends readers forth with encouragement for their future. The qualities of flexibility, openness, and adaptability are cited as those most helpful for success in an evolving and unknown educational future.

None of us knows completely where our careers are leading. All we can really bring into the tomorrows of our teaching are ourselves. The intent of this book is to enable the readers to incorporate into their professional lives self-care, growth experiences, and personal qualities that will best equip them not only to survive whatever comes but to thrive as well. Read on to learn ways to do this and to do it creatively!

MARY ZABOLIO MCGRATH

Acknowledgments

With special gratitude—

To those many educators in the classroom next door, down the hall, in the office, and on the phone who have offered me support and encouragement through all my years of teaching.

To all who have modeled and shown me the importance of self-care.

To my husband, Jim McGrath, for his technical and editorial skills and also his steady support and great patience throughout this project.

To my mother, Dolores Albel Zabolio, for her continued words of encouragement during the writing of this book.

To the staff of the Bloomington Print Shop, especially Luann Barta, for assistance with graphic arts.

To all family, friends, staff, and parents who offered me support in the form of good words, laughter, and prayers throughout the writing process.

And finally, to the Divine potential within that moves us on the journey toward wholeness.

About the Author

Mary Zabolio McGrath has taught both regular and special education classes in elementary and secondary schools since 1969. She is presently teaching emotionally/behaviorally disordered, learning disabled, and mildly mentally handicapped students at Ridgeview Elementary in Bloomington, Minnesota. She completed her doctoral work in 1988, with her dissertation titled *Job Stress and Burnout Among Teachers of the Emotionally/Behaviorally Disordered.*

In addition, she has written pamphlets on teacher stress, which she markets through her small business, Reflections Resources, Inc. She currently writes a column titled "Job Stress Perspectives," published in the *MEEDer Reader,* a state-level publication of the Minnesota Educators of the Emotionally/Behaviorally Disordered. She has given presentations on teacher stress at conventions of the Minnesota Federation of Teachers and the Council for Children With Behavior Disorders (CCBD). She spoke most recently on the topic of administrative support at the Southeastern Regional Conference of the CCBD.

This is her first book.

1

Living With Stress Creatively

In any teachers' lounge, during breaks or at lunchtime, the discussion invariably turns to events of the school day. Conversations progress something like this one, occurring in a suburban elementary school.

"So how's your day going, Sue?" asks Jerry, the phys-ed teacher.

"Well, actually, just about normal," responds the second-grade teacher. "Trent is on an emotional roller coaster. He was at his dad's all weekend and hasn't adjusted to being back with his mother. It usually takes him until Wednesday to make the transition and then he has to go back to his dad's. To add to that, Mandy came without breakfast for the third time this week so I had to take some time hunting down crackers so she would have enough energy to function. Sarah's dad is on an extended business trip so I'm warning you to put on your 'daddy hat' when she comes to class. Our girl is pretty needy right now."

"That sounds like what I've come across today. In my first class, Brian forgot his Ritalin so things were pretty chaotic. Danny's been talking all morning about some TV show he watched late last night. It sounded really inappropriate for kids to me. Laura was complaining about being too tired to play soccer. Her mom started a new job and dropped her off at day care around 6:00 A.M. The job's quite a distance from here so it seems like Laura will stay at her day care until nearly 6:00 P.M."

"This probably isn't the last day she'll be tired!" adds Dina, the social worker, thinking to herself about her morning sessions— a suspected sex abuse case and the child in tears because of a teenage brother on drugs. "These kids really have it tough sometimes."

"And so do we!" quips Sue. Opening the newspaper, she exclaims, "Oh, no, another anti-teacher letter on the opinion page. The writer thinks we make too much money and don't work hard enough!"

An unfamiliar teacher enters the lounge and joins the group.

"Hi, I'm Ron Parker, substitute in fourth grade."

"How ya doin'?" choruses the group.

"Well, actually just great. You have such easy kids to deal with compared to the inner-city schools. I was a secondary administrator there before I retired. Kids today have so many problems and concerns. I had to confiscate weapons regularly. There were a lot of fights . . . not to mention property damage to our school. We didn't have an endless budget either. Class sizes kept going up. Then, of course, we had such a transient population, the composition of some classrooms changed quite a bit by spring. Add in the special education students with all their unique problems. Kids these days have so many needs and it all falls on us. I don't know how teachers do it, day in and day out. I really don't. . . . Anyway, it seems like a pretty nice place to work . . . here in the suburbs."

"Funny you should say that, Ron. I was just thinking that things are getting worse out here!" moans Dina.

Present societal conditions influence schools everywhere to varying degrees. Such factors as those mentioned above, the changing composition of the family, parental neglect, a fluctuating economy, job mobility, sexual abuse, increased criticism of public education, violence, drug and alcohol abuse, and decreased respect for people and property have an effect on classrooms on a daily basis. Today's culture, defined as the current expression of values, relational patterns, societal fragmentation and fractures, pace, and priorities unique to our time, translates into ongoing educational challenges that affect considerably the stress levels of school employees.

Mass media, so prominent in our culture, also affects students today. Not only do they have a grasp of mature subjects at a younger age, but they also are accustomed to being entertained. Consequently, teachers often believe that they have to compete with the television and motion picture industries. Students who spend a lot of time watching television sometimes respond poorly to traditional methods of teaching. They also appear to need a different style of teaching and may require more experiential and hands-on learning. The lecture mode doesn't work with all students. As a result, creating innovative learning situations takes teachers' time and potentially produces stress.

School districts are attempting to address current problems resulting from societal changes. Educational publications report school responses to our economy, such as early intervention programs and subsidized meals for students. We read about teachers who buy many of their own supplies, even textbooks. At the same time, they struggle to pass tax referendums in an effort to maintain quality education. Another attempted solution to social problems is the implementation of specialized curricula, addressing such topics as chemical use and sexual abuse at all grade levels. School-sponsored campaigns to turn off television and replace it with other activities, such as reading or family recreation, are noble efforts to bring more wholesomeness into the lives of students. Public opinion about modern education is addressed by teacher organizations' seeking to put the perspectives of educators into the media and political arena. School personnel who write letters to local newspapers, communicate often with parents, or work with parents on shared school projects hope to better public relations as well. School districts and local communities endeavor to curb violence with such options as stricter discipline codes, violent-intruder drills, conflict resolution training, collaborative community-school violence prevention programs, midnight sports leagues, and job training programs. Within this maelstrom of problems and attempted solutions are those of us who work in schools today, experiencing both the stressful and positive effects of modern education.

Circumstances created by educational institutions, current educational trends, and changing policies affect all educators. Returning to the staff lounge, the conversation of the second lunch shift is just beginning.

> "What a morning!" groans Annie Tyler, first-grade teacher. "That Billy! Oh! He's got to be a candidate for special help. I don't know what to do with him anymore. He's all over the room. The kid just can't pay attention. By the way, I sent him to the principal again today."
>
> "What'd he do this time?" asks psychologist Don Benson.
>
> "I caught him taking a snack out of Andrew's backpack and he looked me right in the eye and said he didn't do it! This isn't the first time he's taken something that wasn't his."
>
> "Yeah, it sounds like you've got a potential candidate for us, all right. Maybe you should start thinking about a referral."
>
> "Oh, those forms, they take forever. Maybe he'll get better."
>
> "Suit yourself, but it sounds like he may get worse."
>
> "Speaking of worse . . . since the district adopted this new reading series, the kids aren't learning as well. I'm worried that a lot of them will qualify for learning disability services by spring."
>
> "Let me know, and I'll do some testing."

Besides cultural factors and their effects on teachers, it is important to note the influence of litigation and educational trends. Special education policy has been largely driven by the results of court cases. Paperwork and entry/exit procedures have become lengthy and cumbersome. Thus students from self-contained special classes who formerly would have been mainstreamed are now totally included in many cases. This remains a challenge to both regular and special educators who must refashion classroom structures. Implementation of new educational models is a difficult, time-consuming, and stressful task.

With new educational models come changing instructional methodologies. Some methods are viewed by teachers as effective and helpful for students. Others are less so, yet teachers are required to use them. Trendy educational fads, according to some teachers, only clutter their curricula and sidestep student needs. When teachers must choose between what they consider sound instruction and what the district requires, only stress can result.

A changing world fosters a rapidly changing curriculum. Teachers struggle with an ever-expanding content. They wonder how they can cover violence prevention, drug awareness, conflict resolution, self-esteem, appropriate touch, and suicide prevention and still teach the required basics—reading, math, and spelling. This is a major stress factor for teachers. So much has been added to the curriculum over the years, and nothing has been taken away. In addition, teachers have been told to cover the curriculum in greater depth with enriched meaning, and the new demands of student-centered learning require longer periods of time to cover the topics. Yet teachers are expected to accomplish all this, and individualize instruction so that all students can achieve the high standards using their own personal learning styles, in the same number of instructional minutes that they had 20 years ago. It simply can't be done, and it is highly stressful to be given a task you know you can't complete.

Has it always been like this? Let's go back to the lounge and listen to what the third lunch shift have on their minds.

"Our lunchroom is so noisy, and the kids are so disrespectful. Throwing food is nothing to them—and the waste!" exclaims Mrs. Santinelli, assistant principal. "When I started as an administrator 40 years ago, I could walk into a secondary lunchroom and they'd quiet down at the sight of me. All I had to do was give them that look, you know. Now I can walk through an elementary lunchroom virtually unnoticed!"

"No kidding!" exclaims Mark, a first-year teacher. "That's so hard to believe. Were kids ever that . . . tame?"

"Things sure were different in my first year of teaching than they are today," notes Elsa, an experienced teacher who often speaks longingly of retirement.

"I bet you didn't know what stress was then," laughs Mark.

"Well, I wouldn't go that far!" Elsa says wistfully. "But sometimes I wish I could board a time machine."

"Well, folks, if you're really interested in the kinds of stress teachers had in the past, I can add some insight to this conversation," interrupts Judy, a fourth-grade teacher. "I'm taking a class at the university, and last week, believe it or not, the instructor talked about how teachers in the 1920s experienced stress."

"Really?" "Hey, now!" "Unreal!" the group says all at once.

"Yeah," she continues, "the study of teachers showed that around 10% of the subjects had experienced a nervous breakdown."

"That was the era of the flappers, speakeasies, and the stock market crash. Hmm. . ."

"If I remember correctly, the prof told us that blame was placed on the changing economy and social conditions of the time."

"Sounds familiar. What else did you learn?"

"Well, during the 1930s, the Great Depression didn't leave the teachers without stress either. He mentioned another national-level survey, which showed that over a third or so of the teachers who participated identified themselves as being seriously worried or nervous."

"What about the 1950s when you were young?" teases Mark.

"So you've guessed my age—ballpark figure, anyway! When I was a little girl, around 20% of the teachers reported that they were working under quite a bit of strain, and over 60% said they were experiencing a fair amount of it."

"You did it to them, Judy!"

"Well, that's not so far from the truth. Their reported causes of stress were class size and the kinds of kids they taught!"

"Oh, no!"

"Oh, yes! Then, of course, he's told us about recent teacher stress research, which is more of the same."

"Then the stress has always been there," says Mrs. Santinelli.

"And always will be," concludes Mark. "Guess I better learn to live with it!"

Stress has affected our forebears in the teaching profession even as far back as the early frontier days when teachers in one-room schoolhouses were faced with starting a wood stove each morning and juggling curriculum for several grades. We in education have shared a common struggle throughout the decades—surviving stress.

In each era, the form of stress has been dealt to us a little differently by the unfolding culture and individual educational systems. Nevertheless, it has existed and remains a challenge for us who face it in its unique form today.

In recent times, to a casual observer, certain teaching jobs could have been considered more stressful than others. At the top of the list of stressful educational settings might have been a self-contained class for the severely emotionally disturbed. Geographically, an inner-city teacher may have been looked on as having it more difficult than colleagues in rural or suburban areas. In terms of levels of service, secondary might have been deemed rougher than primary, middle school or junior high more challenging than kindergarten. Today, when mass media and rapid transit influence and connect our culture, things appear to have evened out somewhat. Studies show and teacher discussions across the land indicate that similarities exist all over. Our stress is far reaching and has a steady influence on educators everywhere. Although each of us is not always at the epicenter of every cultural influence such as gang violence or sexual abuse, we feel the shock waves and reverberations of societal discord daily in our classrooms. Systemic attempts at solutions to social problems have proven to be effective in some instances, whereas in others the teacher is the single warrior on the cultural battlefield. Switching roles in any given day from teacher to counselor, from parent to social worker, from nurse to police officer is not uncommon.

Although sociocultural influences pervade the educational setting of today, typical pressures that teachers have always faced exist as well. These include stresses resulting from policies and issues unique to each school system and those that arise from daily interaction with students, coworkers, parents, and administrators. In the midst of it all, teachers as never before must take into account their own well-being. To do so, the first step is to define stress and examine how it personally affects us on the job.

A Definition of Present-Day Educational Stress

In the context of today's society, educational stress can be defined as the reaction to negative sociocultural and systemic influences that leads to diminished physical and behavioral health. If a teacher is excessively exposed to such influences, stress will increase and eventually lead to burnout. Figure 1.1 is a graphic representation of this definition.

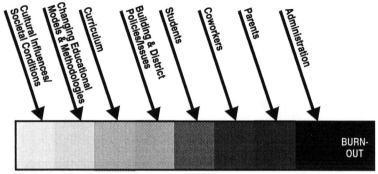

Physical and Behavioral Health

Figure 1.1. Educational Stress

The Stress-Burnout Connection

If educational stressors are not addressed, physical and behavioral symptoms will increase. Educators who typically don't maintain good physical health are more inclined to get sick and experience less energy. They may develop a negative attitude; lose perspective; become more worried, anxious, or withdrawn; and interact less compatibly with coworkers. As symptoms grow in frequency and intensity, burnout eventually occurs. However, with the employment of self-care and personal growth measures, the move toward burnout can be reversed as noted in Figure 1.2.

Unfortunately, when I taught severe EBD students, I did not employ sufficient self-care early enough to prevent burnout. I took a leave of absence to embark on the difficult road back to physical and behavioral health. For me, recovery continued even into my next position. Coming back from burnout was not quick and easy. Personal reconstruction takes time. It is far better to implement self-care early than to have to make the journey around the whole circle.

Creating a Stress Profile

Whether we are general or special educators and work in an elementary or secondary school located in a city, suburb, or rural area, each of us is faced with a personalized set of stressors. Our unique circumstances cannot be trivialized by general solutions, but they can

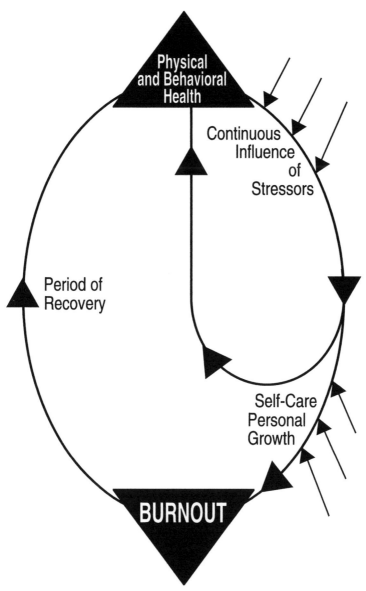

Figure 1.2. Burnout Cycle

at least be placed in similar categories. Having read the descriptions of societal, cultural, and environmental issues, perhaps your job stressors have come to mind. Figure 1.3 contains stress categories common to all educators today. Here you may list those you personally face at the present time.

These four action steps can be used in conjunction with the form shown in Figure 1.3.

1. *Clarify.* The initial step in solving any dilemma is to clarify the areas of concern. Once they are written out in the space provided, you will have created a more objective picture of your present situation.

2. *Prioritize.* Next, highlight those items listed that you consider most important. Prioritizing may target those that you'd like to address first and those you think you can do something about.

3. *Strategize.* With your priorities in mind, your third step is to determine solutions either by yourself or with the help of trusted and supportive coworkers or friends. Others may have experienced similar difficulties and may contribute effectively to you strategy. Perhaps solutions may come to mind as you read through the pages ahead.

4. *Act.* Finally, at the appropriate time, take action. Determine what you can change and do it. Action on those things that you cannot affect may be done in the form of gaining a new perspective on the situation. This can be done through discussion with coworkers who may be experiencing the same thing but view it differently.

Hans Selye (1976), former director of the International Institute of Stress at the University of Montreal, isolated 31 symptoms of stress. Other pioneer researchers have added to the list of symptoms. To simplify matters, a composite of their findings relevant to education is presented here (see Figure 1.4) under two categories: physical symptoms and behavioral symptoms. Both are divided into subcategories, and symptoms ascertained by each researcher are noted accordingly. To determine your symptoms, check or highlight those applicable to you. Place the present date in the space provided.

Then, after you integrate into your life some of the self-care and personal growth suggestions described in this book, reevaluate your-

Cultural influences and societal conditions	Changing educational models and methodologies
Curriculum	Building and district policies and issues
Students	Coworkers
Parents	Administration

Figure 1.3. Personal Job Stressors

self using a pen of another color. It is hoped that no matter how long you wait between measurements, whether it be a quarter, a semester, an entire school year, or more, your next evaluation will indicate an increased ability to live creatively with stress.

Physical Symptoms of Stress
Symptoms Causing Bodily Discomfort
__ asthma *
__ frequent colds *
__ headaches#*
__ menstrual dysfunction#
__ mouth or throat dryness#
__ migraines#*
__ neck/back pain #
__ pounding heart#
__ sweating#
Symptoms Affecting Energy and Endurance
__ dizziness#
__ fatigue#
__ trembling#
__ weakness#
Symptoms Related to Digestion
__ colitis*
__ diarrhea*
__ digestive disturbances#
__ frequent urination#
__ loss of appetite#
__ ulcers*

KEY
Selye (1976)
* Pines as reported by Hendrickson (1979)
+ Maslach and Jackson (1981)
** Freudenberger (1980)
++ Mattingly and Weiskopf as reported by Holland (1982)

Evaluation
Date:_____

Reevaluation
Date: _____

Behavioral Symptoms of Stress
Symptoms Related to Attitude
__ building emotional walls**
__ helplessness+
__ having a negative and cynical regard towards clientele +
__ ineffectiveness+
__ loss of sexual interest*
__ low self concept*
__ questioning the meaning and purpose of teaching*
Symptoms Related to Perception
__ bodily sensations caused by tensing+
__ disorientation +
__ easily startled by small sounds+
__ feeling of unreality+
__ inability to concentrate+
__ sleeplessness#*
__ uneasiness+
Symptoms Related to Mood and Mental Disturbance
__ aggressiveness#
__ anger**
__ boredom**#
__ depression #*
__ despair**
__ floating anxiety#
__ general irritability#
__ hyperexcitation#
__ neurotic behavior#
__ urge to cry or run and hide#
Action-Related Symptoms
__ accident proneness#
__ eating alone++
__ grinding of teeth#
__ high pitched laughter#
__ hypermobility#
__ impulsiveness#
__ leaving early or late to avoid others++
__ missing meetings++
__ skipping breaks++
__ speech difficulties#
__ withdrawing++

Figure 1.4. Symptoms of Stress

2

Taking Charge of
Your Own Self-Care

While exercising at my health club recently, I recalled the first day I tried to run a quarter mile. It was impossible for me, a trim teacher in my early 20s, to make it around a high school track even once. There was no physical reason why I couldn't make that short run. But at that time in my life, even though I made an attempt to eat a fairly healthy diet for weight control, I had little concern for living a balanced lifestyle. I was out of condition, a smoker with irregular sleep habits, and placed minimal emphasis on personal self-care. Comparing my present self-care practices with those of my younger years, I find myself far ahead today.

Over time, I've had the benefit not only of a burnout experience to motivate me into more healthy personal habits but also of the influence and modeling of inspiring individuals who took charge of their own self-care. I wanted to be like them and consequently chose to put effort into making my life path a healthy one. I too decided to take charge of my own self-care.

For those educators concerned about self-care, there is benefit in taking stock of oneself and one's situation to enhance life habits. A thorough review of present behaviors and situations will not only support your efforts to manage job stress but also bring you down the path of wholeness and health.

Included here are 30 areas for personal examination, divided into the following six categories: health-related habits, health enhancers,

enhancers to improve job function, ways to address personal issues, ways to improve relational skills, and suggestions for making job-related changes.

Health-Related Habits—Taking Charge of the Basics

Each day we go through the routines of eating, sleeping, and moving about, often unaware of the quality with which we perform such habitual actions. Although basics such as diet, exercise, and sleep account for a large percentage of any self-care program, they may be largely ignored by the busy educator because they are so commonplace.

Diet

Those of us who have taught health classes are familiar with the four food groups and the importance of eating three square meals a day. Although it is still considered sound nutritional practice to eat three meals a day, the model has gone from a square to a pyramid (see Figure 2.1).

> The Food Guide Pyramid emphasizes foods from the five major food groups shown in the three lower sections of the Pyramid. Each of these food groups provides some, but not all of the nutrients you need. Foods in one group can't replace those in another. No one food group is more important than another—for good health you need them all. As you can see, fat and added sugars are concentrated in foods from the Pyramid tip. These foods provide calories but little or no vitamins and minerals. By using these foods sparingly, you can have a diet that supplies needed vitamins and minerals without excess calories. Some fat or sugar symbols are shown in the food groups. When choosing foods for a healthful diet, consider the fat and added sugars in your choices from the food groups, as well as the fats, oils and sweets from the Pyramid tip. (U.S. Department of Agriculture, 1992)

When we come into the lounge feeling hungry, tired, and stressed, it's so tempting to grab a sweet roll or a few cookies. We can

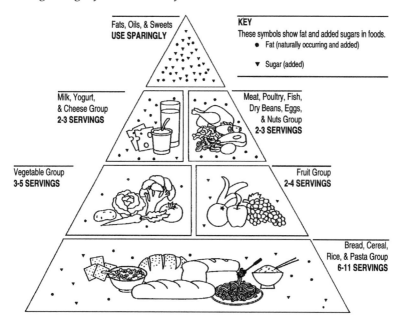

Figure 2.1. Food Guide Pyramid: A Guide to Daily Food Choices
SOURCE: U.S. Department of Agriculture and the U.S. Department of Health and Human Services. Provided by the Education Department of the National Livestock and Meat Board.

easily do this without even thinking, and at times that's OK. Preplanning, however, can assist us in making wiser selections on a regular basis. Teachers who bring their favorite healthy snacks to school are able to avoid everyday lounge temptations, satisfy the need for a snack, and keep their eating habits on track.

Snacks can be selected creatively from any food group. Just use your imagination. When it's your turn to bring a treat, substituting a plate of fruit or vegetables and dip for sugary desserts or greasy chips may be appreciated by more people than you think. You could even become a trendsetter.

Besides lounge treats, some school lunch programs have historically offered us many enticements to eat "fun foods" that smell wonderful but may not be the best for us. The U.S. Department of Agriculture is now issuing regulatory measures to ensure that districts serve more healthy lunches. Many school districts are "taking steps to cut down on salt and fat in the school lunches" and to include "more fiber in the form of vegetables, fruits and grain products" (Owen, 1994, p. 1A). Some have done this for many years. The pyramid is taking hold, and those of us who also eat at school will reap the dietary benefits of such changes along with our students. Until the lunches are revamped, many teachers are opting to buy selectively from the daily menu or bring their own lunches. Some school lunch programs even provide optional choices, allowing staff to make substitutions. For example, on request, the piece of cake listed on the menu may be exchanged for an apple. Thus staff are allowed flexibility in altering their lunch menu.

Teachers who "brown-bag it" often do so because they are attempting to curb weight gain and are following a specified diet. For me, weight gain is a continuous challenge, and I generally follow a specified food plan. In addition, a diet group at my health club has been helpful in assisting me to maintain the weight suggested for my height and age. Currently, I am on a weight control "buddy plan" with another staff member. We weigh in each Wednesday at school and offer encouragement and support to one another throughout the week.

Some teachers I've talked to who are on special diet programs attribute the challenge of weight control partly to stress eating. Reputable weight programs everywhere take into account the factors that cause us to overeat and provide support and encouragement in such matters.

Water

Most diet programs now encourage participants to drink at least eight glasses of water daily for better weight loss. In fact, some teachers keep water bottles right at their desk and sip them throughout the day. Proponents of drinking water have told me that constant hydrating also keeps the body well tuned and claim that they have had fewer colds because of their "drinking habit."

Alcohol

When Friday afternoon arrives, it's not uncommon for teachers to go to a favorite spot for a TGIF (thank goodness it's Friday) gathering. Unwinding together is a pleasant experience and gives many an opportunity to rehash the events of the week. Dealing directly with issues through discussion with colleagues is a healthier way than seeking the oblivion of too much alcohol. Teachers who consider their motivation for drinking choose to limit alcohol intake. Rather than numbing themselves from the stresses of the week by drinking to excess, they limit their alcohol to one or two drinks or order non-alcoholic beer or wine, mineral water, soda, or juice.

Caffeine

A beverage commonly found in schools is coffee. Its pleasant aroma greets us each morning when we enter the lounge, and it is present at staff meetings, conferences, and workshops. Some teachers claim that they need coffee to start the day. Others require its continued usage to keep going until they head for the parking lot at day's end. The jolt of caffeine, whether it comes from the lounge coffee pot, building pop machine, or in a chocolate bar, has become vital for some. I recently overheard a conversation between two individuals in the crowded lobby of a sports arena. One told the other about her experience of going off coffee. Although it was rough at first, she claimed that gradual reduction of coffee and substitution of herbal teas allowed her natural energies to emerge. Like this woman, I have chosen to refrain from caffeine. This stimulant not only causes my hands to shake and produces hurried thoughts in my mind but also prevents me from getting to sleep easily. It affects each person differently and, as with alcohol, many find moderation to be the best guide. The easy access to decaffeinated coffee makes the reduction of caffeine easier for some.

Tobacco

One doesn't have to look far for information on the health hazards associated with tobacco, yet some educators still cling to this addictive habit. When I was a beginning teacher, I enjoyed stepping into the lounge and joining the gang for a cigarette. I looked forward to returning to my apartment where I could "light up" and review the day. Before building restrictions were placed on smoking, it was permitted in teachers' lounges and even at staff meetings. The current trend is to quit smoking, and many teachers are now heeding the warnings and stopping. Those who find it hard to quit on their own are finding support in special programs or using ways recommended by their doctors. They are also discovering that they feel better, look better, and are increasing their capacity to exercise as never before.

Exercise

Teachers today are finding many creative ways to include exercise in their daily schedules. I frequently go to a health club early in the morning. Getting exercise before school makes it a priority and enables me to avoid the traffic delays during morning rush hour. Going there in the early morning also provides me with a quiet time when I can gather my thoughts and plan for the day. Usually when I arrive at the club, a paraprofessional from my building is on her way out the door and an elementary teacher is already swimming laps in the pool. While walking the track, I often notice a member of my school staff vigorously working out on the treadmill. Early morning exercise has become a valued routine for many.

A swimming pool, tennis and racquetball courts, an indoor track, aerobics classes, weights, and exercise machines are among the many choices available to health club members. Choosing from a variety of options keeps exercise from getting routine and boring. Counterbalancing aerobic exercise with the strength training of weight lifting is a commonly selected regimen among club members.

Regular visits to a health club, whether before or after school, provide identification with others seeking to maintain physical fitness through frequent exercise. Getting a mental imprint of these health achievers is a valuable side benefit of exercising in such a setting.

One need not pay club dues, however, to exercise. If the cost of health club membership is a concern, there are other facilities available. Resourceful teachers find many ways to exercise, whether they take out a less expensive YMCA/YWCA membership, use public facilities, or participate in community classes and sports leagues. More and more school districts are negotiating group member rates for employees. If your district hasn't done so, it may be an item worthy of negotiation in a future contract.

School district facilities are another inexpensive option. When I taught at a junior high school, I sometimes used the building swimming pool early in the morning. I also volunteered to chaperon ski trips and received a complimentary tow ticket as well.

Teachers who take graduate classes may be able to take advantage of university facilities. During one winter quarter, I discovered the indoor track at the University of Minnesota and found that running there was a welcome break from below-zero weather.

Our own school property or nearby neighborhoods may also offer prime exercise areas. My school, for example, is located near a nature center. Another teacher and I walk there at least once a week. Watching the birds and noting seasonal changes along the trail have been invigorating and energizing experiences for both of us. On return to the school parking lot, we get into our cars with the events of the workday already far behind us.

When winter days are too cold for extended outdoor walks, my partner and I walk our school halls viewing artwork or displays that go unnoticed during the busy workday. We often enjoy a quick visit with other teachers as we briskly circle through their classrooms, conscious of maintaining our heart rates.

Hall walking is a convenient way to exercise, but some teachers need a change of scene and instead opt for mall walking. In shopping centers, they experience the energy of a crowd and enjoy the distraction found in store windows. Fantasy provided by looking at fashion, jewelry, sporting goods, or furniture displays is dream stimulating. Window-shopping also quickly diverts the mind from school-related matters.

Partner exercise provides accountability and the opportunity to relieve job stress while discussing the events of the day. If you don't have a partner, ask around. Sometimes unlikely people are available for a walk, and a pleasant friendship can develop.

Partner and group exercise easily happens when staff teams compete with one other or against other schools. It's not hard to assemble an exercise group if a prize is available for the team that puts in the most minutes or when building honor is at stake. Some schools even start their own sports teams. Once a member of a staff elementary volleyball team, I enjoyed the physical as well as social benefits of playing with an enthusiastic and motivated group.

What are the benefits of exercise? Teachers who do it on a regular basis find that they have increased energy and stamina. They are living proof of the physical and mental health benefits derived from having an exercise program. Those who include weight training in their exercise routine find that they not only have firmer muscles but also improved posture and a solid feeling of being in control.

Exercise is an effective and popular way to handle the stress in education today. It provides us with a way to release job-related anger and frustration that would otherwise do harm to the body as well as the spirit.

Fresh Air and Sunshine

Teachers who choose to exercise or pursue hobbies such as hiking, fishing, or bird-watching will attest to the physical and mental benefits derived from spending time in the great outdoors. This can be done in every season and any time of the day. The paraprofessional who supervises recess at my school has a healthy glow year-round because of her time spent outside. Fresh air and sunshine can be invigorating and provide joy and pleasure to joggers and observers of nature alike.

Sleep

Nothing makes us more vulnerable to job stress than lack of sleep. It seems that when we are tired and run down, events that wouldn't normally bother us appear bigger and more distressing. On the other hand, rested teachers have ready access to their maximum thinking and problem-solving potential and are able to respond with alertness and creativity to the events of the school day.

Unfortunately, some teachers arrive at school already robbed of their daily energy allotment, going on less than the amount of sleep their bodies require. Each of us knows how much sleep is needed and the effect on the quality of our job performance when we don't get enough.

Besides performance benefits, there are health benefits. In previous years, one of my coworkers missed school regularly due to frequent colds and respiratory ailments. This year, I noticed that her attendance at work improved dramatically, and she displayed a great deal of energy. When I asked what she was doing differently, she admitted placing priority on getting to bed an hour earlier and was pleased to be reaping the results. Preventing illness is a worthy benefit of sleep. When I detect the onset of cold and flu symptoms, I've discovered that a good night's sleep is all I need to arrest the symptoms. The proverb, "An ounce of prevention is worth a pound of cure," applies here. Increased sleep at the body's first signals of oncoming illness often deters a more extended illness and enables a teacher to maintain good work attendance.

Sometimes it's difficult for educators to get the required amount of sleep. We're keyed up from events of the day and often mentally replay them. When that happens to me, I try the "warm milk and cracker" remedy used successfully by my mother when I was a child. If that's not enough, I use an exercise someone once recommended that has been a real asset in calming my busy mind. The exercise involves thinking of five objects in the room one at a time, then listening sequentially for five different sounds. The exercise then progresses to mental focus on five parts of the body touching the bedding. This routine is then repeated using four items, then three, and so on. Often before I get to the last round I've already fallen asleep. If all else fails, read an educational journal. Boredom is a guaranteed sleep inducer!

Lack of sleep is sometimes an intentional choice. On a day when I've deprived myself of recreation, I purposely stay up later to read a good mystery or watch late-night television. I solve my need for play but do so at my own risk, often paying a price the next day.

Coming to school excessively fatigued can be a real setup for drinking too much coffee. Consequently, the caffeine user will be too overstimulated to sleep and a potential negative cycle has begun. When good diet and exercise are put into practice, the need for caffeine is reduced, and sleep will come as a natural result.

Physical Health

Teachers who take charge of the basics prevent illness and experience general good health. Other sound practices to assure continued good health are regular visits to health care professionals. This could be visiting a medical doctor for an annual physical or treatment of common illnesses, having regular dental checkups, or seeing a practitioner of alternative medicine, such as a chiropractor, for aches and pains as well as guidance with vitamins and food supplements. A variety of health care professionals are available today to assist teachers not only with their physical condition but also with other essentials. Their help in finding a suitable diet or exercise routine, or assisting with sleep concerns could be the support you need to take charge of the basics of your own health care.

Health Enhancers

In the realm of health-related self-care are some less-commonly-used yet effective interventions against stress that can be bonuses to educators who take advantage of them. These include massage and relaxation exercises.

Massage

Those of us in the education field do a lot of mental work. Few opportunities exist to clear our overtaxed minds unless we create them. One effective way that some teachers have discovered is massage.

Muscles tighten as a result of situational and mental tension. Unexpressed emotions contribute to muscle contraction as well. By directly working the appropriate muscle groups, massage therapists are able to effectively bring the muscles back to their natural state.

While muscles are letting go, the mind parallels the process and school-related thoughts drift away. Scattered thoughts are reordered, enabling more efficient use of the mind. Busy and numbed bodies are resensitized as energy is redirected and renewed.

Massage is offered at health clubs, the YMCA or YWCA, chiropractic offices, and retreat centers. Some massage therapists, for your convenience, will even come to your home. Many work out of their own homes and thus are able to charge less. My massage therapist offers a package of several massages at a lower rate. That way I am able to keep the cost down and schedule them according to need.

I have found that monthly massages help maintain the areas of my body most predisposed to tension, especially the shoulders. Generally, I try to predict optimally stressful times, such as conference days or workshop week, and then plan accordingly. Occasionally, I get a massage at the beginning of vacation days to facilitate "letting go" of school more quickly. Some consumers of massage therapy listen to their bodies and are spontaneous about when they get a massage. I once met an education professor in my massage therapist's waiting room whose shoulders had responded adversely to what she described as a terrible week. Fortunately, she was able to get an appointment on an "emergency" basis. Restless, stressed, and busy teachers can gain physical, mental, and emotional benefits from massage whenever job stress exceeds the body's tolerance level.

Relaxation Exercises

Opposite of massage therapy are relaxation exercises. In massage therapy, another person is required to assist your tense muscles back to their normal condition. Relaxation exercises, on the other hand, are done by oneself and involve tightening already tense muscles. Deliberately tightened muscle groups will return to a more relaxed state once they are held briefly in a tensed position and then released (*Relaxation Skills Take-Home Tape*, 1974).

Another form of relaxation exercise employs the mind. Sustained mental concentration on a muscle group gives attention to that particular area of the body, and muscles gradually relax (de Mello, 1978).

An effective relaxation exercise is deep breathing. Taking time out for a series of deep, measured breaths impelled by the diaphragm can break tension even as we are leading a class down the hall or monitoring a study period. Simple relaxation exercises can be done anywhere and require little time (Monsein, 1978).

Enhancers to Improve Job Function

Successful job performance can be a prime factor in self-care. Teachers' preexisting skills can be maximized by the employment of job function enhancers, such as the use of time management skills, promptness, efficiency, and organization.

Time Management

Educational personnel have much to accomplish in any given day and little time to waste in order to do so. Having a system of time management integrated into work behavioral patterns can maximize efficiency and also reduce job stress. A key principle in time management is setting priorities for task completion. Making lists and ranking tasks according to importance is done in various ways. Some teachers simply list and numerically prioritize daily tasks, whereas others develop their own systems using an outline format. Teachers who invest in daily planners and even take a class on how to use a planner learn a more complex but efficient coded system for doing this. Whatever method is most comfortable will work effectively for you. More important, however, is that educators set priorities and follow them, checking off listed tasks once they are completed.

Duties may need to be reprioritized as events of the day dictate, and thus flexibility comes into play. Stress is induced when teachers allow themselves to be too busy; without a plan, their thinking becomes scattered and their actions random. Such teachers are reactive to events that occur, soon lose command of the day, and very likely have little control over most situations in which they find themselves.

Another factor in effective time management is consistent use of a calendar. It's important to have a record of upcoming events, not only for each day but also for the entire school year. Begin during workshop week by entering all upcoming events scheduled for the months ahead. That way you can plan accordingly and won't be taken by surprise when building activities occur. As additional events are announced, enter them immediately so they won't be forgotten in the busy days ahead.

It's also important to coordinate personal events with school events. I learned the hard way the importance of keeping a total life calendar. Formerly, I had a calendar provided by the district on which I noted school activities. I kept a personal calendar in my purse for my "life" as well. My reason in doing this was to keep "school at school." The price I paid for this attempt to compartmentalize my life was duplicate planning. Unknowingly, I would schedule a play or committee meeting on a required PTA night and have to reschedule with a friend or organization accordingly. Consequently, I bought a personal planner that I now carry everywhere. When friends invite me to a movie, I am able to rely on my availability for a date without the collision of two calendars!

When considering time management and planning for both job-related events and personal events, teachers are sometimes tempted to forgo personal plans for school-related tasks, student performances, and athletic events. Keeping a balance here is important for stress management. Teachers who are able to minimize work-related tasks in the evening are those who return to the job refreshed the next day, reenergized for what lies ahead.

Efficiency and Organization

Although successful attempts have been made to teach time management, efficiency and organization are not skills acquired by attending a short seminar. Teachers generally develop these behaviors through trial and error over time. One way that I've acquired skills in this area is by watching coworkers. I marvel at the organization and efficiency of some of my colleagues. If you feel that you'd like to grow in these areas, just look around. There is on-the-job training in efficiency and organization occurring daily at your school. Efficient and organized teachers do their paperwork with deliberation and concentration. They often attend to a task mentioned on a memo immediately, as opposed to putting it off. Their desks are organized and they have a designated spot, whether it be a special corner or a basket, for placing incomplete work. They delay going to the office or resource center until they have accumulated enough items to make the trip worthwhile. They have proven routines for repetitious and ordinary tasks, such as correcting papers or filling work folders. Once they begin a task, they deliberately see it to completion, as opposed to beginning many tasks and sporadically working on them all at once. Their units and teaching materials are filed in an easily accessible and systematized manner. Daily schedules and expectations for student behavior are posted prominently in their classrooms, giving students as well as themselves a sense of direction for each day. Organization and planning time, such as desk cleaning and personal scheduling time, is provided for students as well. Students' work is prominently displayed, not only for acknowledgment of their successes but also to avoid the work that elaborate bulletin boards require. Commercially produced letters and posters fulfill this purpose in many classrooms. More examples of efficiency and organization can be discovered by watching coworkers and even asking them how they do it. I have learned a great deal this way and discovered that teachers are very willing to share their "secrets of success."

Promptness

The old saying, "The early bird gets the worm," can easily apply in educational settings. Teachers who arrive at school before the required time often are able to prepare adequately for the upcoming day and socialize a bit. Thus they are able to greet students in a relaxed rather than frantic and harried manner. Those who arrive at staff and committee meetings 5 to 10 minutes ahead of schedule find themselves easily making the transition from a previous situation to the present agenda. Having given themselves time to "switch gears," they are able to bring with them the clear and organized thinking that comes from preparedness.

Punctuality is a signal to other team and committee members that you have something to contribute and that you value their contributions as well. Late arrival to a meeting puts you at a disadvantage. Not only do you miss what has already been said, but the distraction of your delayed entry disrupts the thoughts and discussions of those already present.

Promptness in meeting deadlines can also enhance job function and decrease job stress. It is important to break down large projects, listing all aspects of each task, and allot sufficient work time to complete everything. Nothing is worse than the last-minute panic caused by poor planning. Giving up an entire weekend to do reports can only contribute to the stress that accompanies major school projects. Teachers who, on the other hand, make provisions on their calendars for doing necessary paperwork not only meet required deadlines but often do so in a relaxed and thoughtful manner. They are able to be spontaneous and even take advantage of social situations during this time. Because they've planned ahead, they know they will easily complete the required task.

Working It Out—Ways to Address Personal Issues

Difficult work situations in which we find ourselves often require careful consideration and thought in order to be improved. These are not only due to the persons or situations we consider stressful but may be partly self-induced.

Self-reflection and examination of work situations are beneficial in stress reduction. This reflection is enhanced by the knowledge and expertise of others, whether they be writers, people with similar issues, or educational and mental health professionals.

Self-Help Literature and Tapes

An abundance of material is now available for purchase or obtainable in public libraries on topics of self-help and personal growth. Relative to teacher stress can be other factors in the life of an educator, whether from the past or present. Myriad books and tapes addressing such topics as chemical dependency, dysfunctional families, anger, relationships, or marital communication can be of great assistance in working out such issues.

Journal Writing

A common means of expression and a helpful way to work out unspoken feelings is journal writing. The journal is a safe place to unload daily frustration and say the unthinkable. Anything goes in a journal. Once intense emotions are expressed and puzzling situations become clearer, teachers can more easily address the challenging realities of their work settings.

Growth Workshops

Commonly associated with workshops is the acquisition of new ways to teach reading, math, or social studies. Often teachers set aside time in the summer to improve their knowledge in a preferred subject area. In addition, teachers take advantage of workshops addressing subjects of personal growth. The benefit of attending such workshops is the identification with others who have a similar personal history or self-help needs. Presentations, material, guided activities, and group discussions offered in such workshops can help a participant sufficiently address issues of concern. On the other hand, workshops of this nature can generate more questions and open up related issues that will require further and more specific help.

Self-Help Groups

Some years ago, extensive inservice in chemical dependency was given to the staff in my school district. As a result of the valuable information presented by professionals and the guided discussions that followed, staff not only received more education on the subject of alcohol and drug abuse, but some also uncovered memories of family alcoholism and abuse long suppressed.

Consequently, participants, motivated by the workshop, sought to work further on personal issues in 12-step groups such as Alcoholics Anonymous (AA), Al-Anon, or Adult Children of Alcoholics. There are groups available for just about any addiction or concern imaginable. The confidentiality factor required in these groups makes them safe places where teachers can share family history and personal pain with others who understand. By the nature of our jobs, we in education are placed in the role of helper and have to be the ones who "have it all together." And naturally, it is unwise to share problems of such a personal nature in the staff lounge and with coworkers. In 12-step groups, all participants are on equal footing, and members provide understanding and support to one another that is not available anywhere else.

Education personnel who attend self-help groups regularly are able to maintain the emotional balance needed to perform their jobs effectively. They are able to address not only family issues at their group meeting but also job-related issues. Attending recovery groups can be a professional and personal advantage to educators. Having grown in personal awareness and understanding of the lives of group members as well, they are better able to relate to the problems and varied circumstances in the lives of parents and students with whom they work.

Professional Help

Teachers are not immune from difficult family backgrounds, marital problems, and vulnerability to challenging personalities. Like individuals in other careers, we experience personal problems with which we need extra assistance. Mental health professionals are widely available for counseling in a variety of matters, whether it be to address patterns formed due to our family histories or work-related situations. Some school districts provide employee assistance programs, often through an outside company. These are offered as one of the fringe benefits and are accessed in the form of a telephone help line or, more long term, in the form of trained counseling professionals who can help employees with personal problems, ranging from financial stress to rebellious teenagers to caring for an elderly parent. A trusted social worker, psychologist, or psychiatrist can also be accessed through physician referral, and these are usually included in school health insurance plans. If such benefits are not available, teachers should negotiate for them.

Acting It Out—Ways to Improve Relational Skills

Education is a field in which professionals are quick to take action on behalf of students. Educators do not always address their own needs and concerns as readily. Professional relationships among school personnel can be challenging, and issues occur that require individual action on a day-to-day basis. The following are suggestions to better our professional relationships. When things are going smoothly among staff members, stress is minimized for all involved.

Communication

Organizational communication travels in two ways. The first is through formal means such as school bulletins, staff meetings, and performance reviews. Another and often-faster way is through the informal network or "grapevine" (Goldhaber, 1979). Real news as well as rumor travels this way. Characteristically, in schools, the information traveling on the grapevine is "hot news," gossip, or that which hasn't been properly expressed to the person who really needs to hear it. For example, complaints about a new policy suggested at a staff meeting travel quickly on the informal network, whereas little might have been said in honesty about it to the principal when it was announced. Such indirect expression can have lethal consequences in a building. Sweeping issues "under the rug" keeps them unresolved. Negative attitudes perpetuated by such communication dynamics spread through a building like a virus. The end product is a dysfunctional and unhealthy school organization.

Why don't educators choose the straight route to address their concerns and express their emotions? They may have developed a habit of false politeness. In my state, we refer to it as "Minnesota nice." Those practicing this behavior would never consider saying anything controversial for fear of offending someone.

Fear may be another cause of indirect communication. It can be frightening for some to express their true opinions or honestly confront a coworker. Fear tells us that direct confrontation will result in ill will. It further convinces some educators that it could be very hard to work with someone day in and day out once they've expressed what they really think about a common concern. Thus the safest response for some may be either to say nothing or to say it to someone else. That way, they reason, no one will be offended.

In contrast, I recently witnessed a courageous teacher state his concerns clearly at a staff meeting. He publicly took ownership of his frustration regarding latecomers to his class and asked for suggestions. He then fielded a discussion of ways the group could better assist him in avoiding this problem in the future. The teachers were then able to tell him why it might be difficult for them to meet his request, and a constructive discussion resulted. Instead of sitting at the meeting with a knot in his stomach, complaining later to another coworker, or going home and griping to his wife, this teacher raised his concerns with those who could help resolve it.

Once a skill is learned and developed, the fear will decrease. Figure 2.2 shows a simple formula for direct expression that is increasing in popularity among teachers. It has been used in our school district for conflict resolution training, and those who use it are finding it very helpful and constructive for both adult-adult and adult-student interactions (Citizens Council Mediation Services, 1994).

At one point in my career, I encountered a teacher heading for the principal's office. She said, "I've got to say this. It's been building up inside me for days and I'm going to say it! It's scary but I'm going in there and finally say how I feel." This teacher had communication skills and was developing them. Each time we attempt to be honest and to be so in a constructive way, we increase our confidence as capable communicators, benefiting ourselves and our schools.

Assertion Without Blaming

I feel _____

when you _____

because _____

(and\or "and I want _____ ").

Figure 2.2. "I" Statement
SOURCE: Citizens Council Mediation Services (1994). Used with permission.

Assertiveness

The simple formula in figure 2.2 is one of many examples of assertive communication. Those choosing to be assertive are choosing the middle ground. On one end of the communication continuum are those who never stand up for themselves, whether it be out of fear, a sense of unworthiness, or lack of skill. These educators live with a belief system that says they are unworthy of having their needs met and concerns addressed. Others in this category take the philosophy of "If you want to get along, go along" to an extreme. Regardless of what opinions they hold or feelings they experience, they do not risk expressing them, believing they have too much to lose if they do so. Such educators often mask their true feelings behind a smile or a nod, even though inside they may be ready to explode. Never having stood for anything at a staff meeting or on their teaching team, such teachers may have lost touch with their own ideas and emotions, not allowing themselves even privately to think about or internally experience them. On the other end of the continuum are teachers who are aggressive. Vocal and demanding, they seek to control their situations. They often dominate discussions and intimidate anyone who dares to disagree with them. Coworkers and administrators find it easier to give in to their requests rather than engage in any discussion with them because they will often go to any measure to have things their way.

Balanced between these extremes is the assertive educator. These individuals have developed appropriate communication skills and are aware of their needs, desires, and feelings. They have a good sense of self-esteem and therefore believe they deserve to be heard. Having self-respect, they do not tolerate rude or thoughtless behavior from anyone in the workplace. Even though they may feel uncomfortable and even scared to stand up for themselves, they do it anyway because they would experience a sense of being robbed of personal integrity if they didn't. Such educators care enough about coworkers that they call forth respectful and mature behavior from them. Those who disagree with assertive educators often respect them for taking a stand. Assertive educators can be trusted because they communicate openly and directly in all their work relationships.

Anger

Those of us in education think of ourselves as generally congenial, caring people. Anger is something we comfortably allow ourselves to direct at unruly students. Yet in regard to adults, we may not always be certain how to handle it. When anger is expressed, it commonly comes out as complaining and whining about something a parent said or an administrator did. Indirect expression of anger is relatively common in education. The angry educator talks about a perceived hurt or injustice with everyone but the person who is the source of the concern. Consequently, the relationship is never repaired, and opportunity for resentment is great. Such anger cannot be easily defused and, like unexpressed anger, it goes into the system and affects everyone, leading to a negative building atmosphere.

Often teachers are angry about a recent school or personal event and respond in various ways. Sometimes they keep it to themselves. This is common in schools run by administrators using an autocratic, more authoritarian style of management. When teachers are treated as children, they rarely express their opinions let alone their angry feelings. The anger is present, though, and contributes to an already oppressive building atmosphere. This unaddressed anger goes into a building's social system, sits there, and festers. Teachers working under these conditions become blank in facial affect and inward in emotional expression. They give up easily and may take the anger out on themselves. The result is physical illness, depression, or dullness of spirit.

Another option is to deal directly with the anger. This can be done in the following ways:

Write it out. One can gain a more objective vantage point in regard to a source of anger when it is described in a journal. I keep a notebook in my desk for the exact purpose of letting out my concerns. That way, I can examine the situation that caused my anger and get the feelings out on paper. Because the anger is being processed, the chance of snapping at students or coworkers is decreased. If something is still "eating at me" when I leave school, I may do additional writing at home in the evening. One technique that I've learned is to assemble the participants mentally in a situation of concern and write out a dialogue of their potential thoughts and ideas (Progoff, 1983). That way, I can better understand everyone's viewpoint and bring some resolution to the situation. Amazingly, when I see these individuals the next day, I feel as if we are closer to resolving our differences.

Work it out. If I can't find the time to quickly write in my journal while I am at school or if I've written in my journal and still feel intense anger, I then try to release it physically. I was once told that the four ways to release anger are hitting, kicking, biting, and screaming. The only one suitable for the ride home is screaming. Have you ever "let it all out" in the car with the radio blasting? Try it sometime. Fellow travelers on the road will just think you're singing! This helps release the "steam" held inside and intensified during the school day. In the privacy of your automobile, you can say anything and everything! I find that if I get involved in name-calling while in the car, it only increases the very anger that I am trying to release. Instead, phrases like "Mrs. Jones, I really feel angry about . . ." help defuse my anger more quickly. Once I reach home, if I still need to rage about a school incident, there's always hitting (a pillow or punching bag, of course). Biting is either too food related or out of the question because I haven't yet found a socially acceptable way to do it. Some students use this mode of expression, however!

Ritualize it. Once angry feelings are expressed on paper, they can be further released through ritual. Angry monologues or dialogues can be burned, ripped up, shredded, or tossed away. The anger expended in ripping also contributes to release. Watching smoke rise in the fireplace gives me a sense of peace as my angry words burn up before me.

We may encounter other angry educators daily. Some are able to handle and address anger-inducing school situations and others are not. Some are even carrying old anger from as far back as childhood, and it shows in the tone of their personality. These educators have "short fuses" and unpredictably respond in anger when most people would not. When a situation occurs that calls for legitimate anger, they may respond with greater intensity than others. These people can be mean-spirited, and working with them is difficult. It's often hard for them to deal openly and honestly with school concerns. Although these individuals are often well-intentioned and sincere people, they are unaware of the effect their actions have on those around them. Personality issues such as these take work and sometimes require professional assistance. However, those willing to look beneath their anger and deal with whatever emotional wound is causing it can grow greatly and become fuller and more amiable professionals.

Boundaries

Besides anger, other expressed and unexpressed emotions, thoughts, and opinions circulate on the communication networks of school. In any given day, an educator is party to an array of feelings and ideas experienced and expressed by coworkers, administrators, parents, and students. There is so much to consider, and one needs to separate those feelings and ideas that are their own from those that belong to others. Healthy educators are able to do this either consciously or unconsciously. They are able to consider whether something is also their issue or concern when a coworker unloads emotions and attitudes in the lounge. Educators without good boundaries take in all these expressions of feeling. They even take up the cause of a coworker as if it were their own and advocate in that regard with others. When unexpressed emotions are "in the air," those lacking appropriate boundaries move into the same mood. For example, when a coworker is depressed, they feel the identical emotion and respond accordingly.

A sample of helpful self-talk to use when confronted with a variety of intense emotions is the following. "Nancy feels angry because the principal asked her class to use the side entrance after recess. That concerns her greatly. Is it my issue? Does it involve me?" If the answer is no, let go and put your energy into what does concern you.

Educators working so closely together with intense and serious problems on a daily basis are also vulnerable to overconcern for everything that faces them in a given day. It's sometimes hard to realize that we cannot change the entire world. When we try to take on too much, especially concerns that are not ours, we end up feeling overstressed and become ineffective. It works best to deliberately choose and prioritize those things that we can effectively influence and disregard or minimally address those things over which we have little or no control. For example, a special education teacher in my district is often overwhelmed with the requests and concerns of classroom teachers. Her favorite response to them is, "I appreciate and understand what you're feeling. This is what I can do for you." She not only directly sets limits with her coworkers but also expresses and validates their emotions, while shielding herself from taking ownership of them.

Another aspect of setting boundaries is the determination of job roles. Educators who work closely together on a daily basis often lose sight of whose duties are whose. Roles start to blur together. It's wonderful when everyone works as a team and willingly jumps in to assist and cover for one another. However, resentment can begin if one worker has expectations of another that are not mutually agreed on. Clarification of roles and duties can prevent the stress and potential conflict that could result from workload imbalance. This takes little time and could prevent misunderstandings among otherwise compatible and congenial coworkers.

Besides setting boundaries in regard to workload, it is also important to consider doing so in regard to interpersonal relationships. As we work together closely on a daily basis, friendships can develop in which educators share deep and personal things about themselves. Personal sharings between trusted school friends can better take place on the telephone or in social situations apart from school. The workplace is not the setting for broad-based self-disclosure, and much of this information is not germane to the task at hand. Something intended to be a personal exchange between two parties could leak out inadvertently and come back to haunt both parties who shared the information. Not only is the grapevine a potential vehicle to carry aspects of our private lives, but it can also distort details and create gossip. Each of us has his or her own level of comfort with regard to what we share at work. Once you've found yours, stick to it. You will avoid the stress of being the subject of school district gossip or the shame and embarrassment of betraying a coworker.

Power

Like communication, power can be held both formally and informally. In some buildings it comes from the top down, and in those using shared decision-making models it is exchanged laterally. Nevertheless, whether someone has been placed in a position of power and leadership or he or she is an employee at a lower level, that person can use power and influence in an organization.

How is this done? Teachers can exert power in every situation by having a clear inner understanding of what they want to do and how they want to do it. Speaking and acting on their educational beliefs casts them as respected leaders in their school. Coworkers not only admire their abilities and professional expertise but seek to imitate them and follow their proven successful methods and practices.

Genuine power does not come from intimidation and control tactics but from professional competence and personal integrity. This holds true for administrators on every rung of the organizational ladder and for other workers as well. Determined educators in all positions can be powerful in their wisdom and professional expertise.

Educators who possess true power have a strong and unwavering sense of professional identity. I once experienced ongoing challenges from a persistent parent. The series of exchanges between us lasted for several months, and I found my confidence wavering. I expressed my uncertainty about the phrasing I had used in a report for that parent to a paraprofessional who assisted me with typing. She simply stated, "Remember, Mary, you're the professional." Power means keeping that fact in mind in all our dealings.

Personal power also means maintaining a true sense of reality. We in education are continuously subjected to criticism from all sides. It does no good to join our critics and distort our own professional competence. It's something we have to believe in whether we experience external affirmation or not. One of the finest teachers I know had a difficult year with a new student. According to written records, the child had behavior problems in a previous setting, yet no one gave the teacher verbal validation of that reality. Consequently, the teacher began to perceive that the child's misbehavior was a professional failure. I was a party to these diminished self-perceptions, and even though I hold this teacher in high regard, I too began to wonder. It was a great thrill for me to hear parental praise given to this educator at the end of the school year, confirming a reality we had both begun to doubt.

A true sense of reality must be maintained even in face of specific criticism. Once an administrator pointed out an area where I needed to grow as a teacher. I knew the criticism was coming and that it was valid. Sometimes I allow personal criticism to color my whole self-perception. To prevent that from happening, right before I met with the administrator, I mentally reviewed successes I'd had throughout my teaching career. Occasional mistakes do not negate the fact that across the board and over the years, all of us have helped many students and parents.

If we lose that reality, whether it is because we are in an unaffirming system or because we face direct and valid criticism, we can recapture a sense of our professional competence either directly from a trusted coworker willing to refresh our memory or from notes we've saved from grateful parents and complimentary administrators.

Power comes with knowing our profession and practicing it with consistent excellence as best we know how. Such an educator will never have to calculate how to climb the organizational ladder. Influence on people and events will come about naturally regardless of your educational position.

Goal Setting

Powerful teachers have a strong sense of self, a sound grasp of reality, and a clear sense of direction. Many who know where they are going professionally do so because they have set definite professional and personal goals. They give their goals priority and allow no one to sidetrack them with an alternative or irrelevant agenda.

Books and tapes are on the market showing interested persons how to develop and attain their goals. Common among the many methods is the importance of writing out goals, reviewing them frequently, and holding oneself accountable for goal attainment.

Although there is much information available about formal goal setting, some people decide to personalize the process and develop their own system. One January, I set aside some time and decided what categories I wanted for my goals. I chose these seven categories: intellectual, personal, spiritual, professional, emotional, physical, and social. I then listed goals under each category and, like New Year's resolutions, made them for the upcoming year. I also made another list of long-term goals for each category. From time to time throughout the year, I reviewed my goals and the following January checked off the ones I had met and revised them for the next year. It has been rewarding to gradually realize the accomplishment of goals over time. I also came to understand that some of my goals were unrealistic, whereas others became irrelevant and unimportant. Nevertheless, those goals that did come into being became the factors that defined my life.

As time went on and I became more comfortable with goal setting, like a true special education teacher who has written many individual educational plans (IEPs), I figured out my percentage of mastery, aiming for 80%. My score gave me an indicator not only of successes but also of areas needing either more effort or discontinuance because they were no longer important. In addition, I now keep my goals in my planner and carry them with me. Whenever I'm feeling off course and tossed about by outside expectations, I review my goals and resolve to renew control over the direction of my life.

Whatever system is used, whether professionally or personally developed, simple or complex, a goal plan can give educators a sense of direction and control over their own destinies. The self-mastery and personal empowerment gained from goal setting diminishes the stress that occurs when we behave as reactive educators without life direction rather than proactive professionals with identity and direction.

Making Job-Related Changes

Taking action, whether through development of communication skills, trying new behaviors, or setting goals, presupposes change. Change can be something that happens to us, and sometimes we have no control over it. At other times, we can bring about change that is not only beneficial to our careers but also is a creative contribution to our survival as educators. The following are examples of minor and major changes we can make.

Our Physical Environment

Whether we realize it, we have the power to influence the environment in which we find ourselves. Primarily, we can change our physical surroundings by placing familiar, comforting, or calming objects and photographs on our desks. It's common to see travel souvenirs, meaningful art objects, or family photographs on the desks of school personnel. Some hang posters or tack up motivational quotes near their work area. Keeping an inspirational book at hand is helpful for some.

The environment can be further changed by rearranging a classroom or enlisting team members in the reorganization of shared space. Again, it's important to use "I" statements to express to office mates or teammates what you would like for a room arrangement and why. They may have their own preferences and needs, and together you can negotiate an arrangement suitable for all. Recently, I began to feel that the space I share with six other special educators was becoming crowded and cluttered. Among us, we share a variety of materials and furniture. It got to a point that I was feeling frustrated and angry. Therefore, at our end-of-the-year housekeeping meeting, using the "I" statement communication formula, I was able to express my thoughts and feelings about our room arrangement. Together we came up with a workable solution, which included sharing desks, rearranging and removing extraneous furniture, and thinning out our supply of materials. Not only do we now have adequate space, but at the suggestion of one team member, we have also created a special area to be used specifically for conferencing and testing. Although I was somewhat afraid to bring up the topic, I was less comfortable living with the growing resentment inside me regarding our previous room arrangement. Using an assertive strategy, I was able to initiate discussion and subsequently effect change in my physical work space.

Influencing the arrangement and housekeeping of shared space can be challenging. Generally, cleaning duties are assigned for the staff lounge. Those wishing to further clean, decorate, or brighten such spaces often work as a committee to take on such tasks as cleaning the refrigerator or buying posters or tablecloths to further improve lounge atmosphere.

There are other ways of changing the physical environment to enhance self-care. I've observed the use of many successful means. One teacher in our building plays Caribbean, easy-listening, and uplifting tapes in her automobile both before and after work. Others beat stress by listening to jazz, high-energy music, or religious radio in their cars. Another listens habitually to classical music on an old radio brought from home. Her classroom is always a pleasant stop for me when I make my after-school rounds to check on special education students.

Sound isn't the only influence on us. Light affects us as well. Before our room was rearranged, I placed my work table near the window. Daylight and a pleasant view always brought me cheer during a long workday. When I stayed late, I enjoyed watching the peaceful sunset as I did tedious paperwork. When my desk was located in a dark corner, I bought a special halogen lamp to brighten my space. It was a worthwhile investment for me at the time. Now that my desk is again away from a window, our building custodian has offered to give me special bulbs known not only to improve lighting but to influence mood as well.

Mood can be affected by color. Bright colors can be energizing and soft colors, calming. Take your pick for the desired effect. A coworker who had a class of severely emotionally disturbed primary students swore by the calming effect of her pink bulletin boards.

For some, fresh air and pure water are a priority. They appreciate the effect of an open window or in colder weather an air purifier. I've frequently taken Wisconsin well water to school in a plastic jug. If I run out, there's always the water filter attached to the faucet in our school nurse's office.

Those who are allergic may react to paint or carpeting in their school buildings. I recently heard of a situation in another school district where several teachers were having similar health problems. Together they got the Occupational Safety and Health Administration (OSHA) involved, and as a result of a building inspection, the carpeting was removed the next day!

Affecting Our Work Setting

The environment that we can change at work is not only in the physical realm but also in our building and classroom atmospheres. Specialists who travel from building to building in a day attest to the differences in the buildings they visit. Some claim that they can sense the climate in a building, whether positive or negative, as soon as they walk in the door.

The composite attitude of all individual staff members creates a building climate. I am responsible only for myself, but collectively we can make a difference. When working in a building that has a negative climate, two teachers can team up and decide not to "buy in to the system" by perpetuating the negativity. You can start your own "positive underground" and eventually add other staff to your numbers. Those trying this may not make major changes, but the team effort can contribute to your own survival.

Working in a negative building or department or on a negative team can seem overwhelming. Finding small islands of comfort can be helpful. Some teachers do it by shutting their doors to keep out negativity. In the privacy of their own classroom, they can use "emotional temperature control." Others seek out pleasant and positive coworkers in the lounge and at lunch, avoiding negative people as much as possible. Positive teachers, teams, and departments can have a work environment on their own terms by being creative.

Classroom climate is largely determined by the teacher. His or her attitude is reflected in the children. Teachers who are firm, fair, and consistent generally are able to create a positive and comfortable classroom climate. Each teacher develops a personal style over time. Yet among the range of teaching styles can be found happy, secure children learning in a positive climate. Teachers can be loyal to their particular styles of teaching and discipline methods and still grow in this area. Workshops and books are available for those needing to learn "new tricks" to contribute to the improvement of their classroom atmospheres.

One person cannot change an entire building. But in many instances, an individual educator can improve his or her own physical and emotional environment by making only minor modifications.

Lifestyle

Many of us in education fall prey to the hectic pace of contemporary living. Balancing the demands of school and home is no easy task in present society, and we often create lifestyles that keep us on a constant treadmill.

Teaching is a female-dominated profession. Over time, I've observed women who have a full-time teaching job assuming both the responsibilities of their jobs as educators and the responsibility for their homes and families. They cook, clean, and chauffeur their children to sports activities and still manage to correct papers and do reports. They are often overwhelmed by the enormity of the task.

My friend Jane, who teaches in a nearby school district, models for me an admirable balance of managing both school and home. She maintains the mindset that her children need her more in their formative years. To her, this time of intense involvement with her children is a temporary and relatively short season of her life. Consequently, during this time, she has chosen to decrease involvement with friends, limiting herself to one outing a month. Jane also builds personal time into her daily schedule by setting aside a half hour daily to watch the news and using her nightly hot bath as her quiet time. Although she loves to read, she defers involvement with best-sellers until summer when she has more available free time. Jane plans to expand her social and personal time when her children are older and more independent. Until then, she follows a consistent and disciplined lifestyle pattern. It's not uncommon for her to work alone in her classroom during lunch so she can leave at a regular time to pick up her children at a nearby day care center and spend some time with them each day. She and her husband go 50-50 on sharing household and child-rearing duties. They work as a team and equally divide grocery shopping, running errands, and playing games with their children. She has described Saturdays around their house as a "work camp" where everyone pitches in to complete tasks. Because this got too grueling, they eventually hired someone to assist with housework. Jane enjoys her professional and her family jobs but admits that doing both well requires effort, family cooperation, personal discipline, and some outside assistance.

Teachers who are single parents face an even greater challenge in keeping their balance. My friend Marie teaches at a vocational college in a nearby state. She recently completed a master's degree while maintaining a teaching job and continuing to raise her two daughters. This is something that Marie would never have been able to accomplish single-handedly. She manages to balance her job, housework, and family commitments through the assistance of a supportive extended family as well as a prayer group and social friends. When necessary, she takes a sick day, goes on a retreat, or visits out-of-town friends to meet her personal and adult relational needs.

Things go best for me when I'm on schedule with all my tasks both at home and at school. Then I am more relaxed and present in both places. However, if I allow the demands to pile up on both fronts, I feel like I'm going from job to job with no break. Whether I "have time" or not, it's important for me to carve out a few hours to prioritize and complete home and school duties. If necessary, I set a timer or take the phone off the hook and get at household duties. When I was single, I hired a cleaning service when things got away from me at home. Now that I'm married, my husband, who has a flexible schedule, assumes a good share of the cooking and cleaning during my teaching months. When the treadmill becomes the norm, it is my signal to make lifestyle changes to reestablish personal equilibrium.

Leaving a Setting

When both managing a home and holding a teaching job get to be too much, some teachers decide to take a family leave. This is especially helpful during the years when they have infants or small children to care for. Part-time jobs or job-sharing arrangements work well for teachers closely involved with young children. Some teachers take jobs as paraprofessionals or use their teaching skills as tutors or substitutes with the intention of returning to full-time work when their children are grown. Others, for economic or professional reasons, rely on periodic holiday breaks and summer to keep both school and home in balance.

Child rearing is not the only reason why teachers leave a setting. They need a change of venue for a variety of reasons. Perhaps they have taught the same grade or subject for many years and are discovering that they have grown a bit stale in the sameness of it all. To regain some spark in their teaching, they switch grades, teams, departments, or buildings. Maybe they are placed in a building with a negative atmosphere or have a principal whose management style and philosophy are in conflict with their own. They could be teamed with individuals they find difficult to work with or want to work in a different neighborhood or specialized school. These are all valid reasons to transfer.

Teachers in difficult situations may have to take some extraordinary measures to survive until they are able to find a new position in a satisfactory location. This could include outside counseling or even temporary medication for stress if it is so warranted. In transferring, they also may have to be willing to take a different type of position. This could bring new challenges as well as opportunities. When I once made a voluntary transfer into a new position, additional training was required for me to retain the new job. Consequently, I began graduate school and met many wonderful people in my new situation.

Arranging an intradistrict transfer is not always easy. It's helpful to have a friend in another building or department who can advocate for you. Union contacts may also be of assistance. Tactfully informing friends and acquaintances of your interest could be of great help.

Perhaps you know an administrator in another building who can assist you in a transfer. One teacher told me of a period in her life when her husband was transferred to a distant city. She took a 1-year leave of absence and when she returned was placed in another building. The school was not to her liking, and she claims that her fervent prayer was "Get me out of here, God!" She called her former principal, offering to take any available opening. Eventually, through the assistance of this administrator, her prayer was answered and she was again placed in her former building.

We know the difficulty of finding jobs in other districts, yet some teachers have managed to make the change. When a spouse transfers, they find new positions and learn much from working in another district. Others choose to independently move to another state or country to pursue a teaching position. Some teachers needing a change have received help from placement organizations and obtained jobs as far away as the Orient and South America. Such assistance, available through the military, teacher exchange programs, and religious organizations, provides teachers with unique opportunities for change in job location both locally and abroad.

Sabbaticals are another option for rest and recuperation from our present positions. Teachers fortunate enough to obtain them have done many creative things, including traveling, studying in another location to enhance their present job, retraining for another form of educational work, and doing independent studies of their own choosing. Sabbaticals have been a means of refreshment for many and are well worth consideration for weary educators needing a change of scene.

Leaving the Profession

Sometimes a temporary change of setting is not sufficient to recover from the ill effects of a difficult teaching job. For some, a career that was once enjoyable and meaningful may become too difficult, stressful, or even mundane, and, consequently, they choose to leave education.

During job change transition, former teachers may engage in a variety of volunteer and paid jobs, many of which are simple and less taxing mentally. A friend and former professor from a prestigious eastern women's college enjoyed her months cleaning houses and working at McDonald's. The pressure was gone and she found her new coworkers to be fun and friendly companions as she searched for her next career. Teachers in transition may also choose the diversion of volunteering in alternative settings, such as nature centers or animal shelters. Meaning can be found in less stressful places than the classroom.

Teacher organizations, community education centers, and churches offer support and retraining for those making career changes. Former teachers have many marketable skills that would be advantageous to them as they seek new employment. Such strengths as oral and written communication, a broad educational background, varied professional training, and seasoned "people skills" can be presented to potential new employers. Former teachers have found successful new careers in business, the arts, skilled labor, journalism, sales, and human resources. The possibilities are many.

When my walking partner and I have had a particularly bad day, we often ask ourselves what we would do if we could change careers. Then we let our imaginations loose and describe old and new career fantasies that include working as forest rangers or in a quiet library. Kernels of such dreams may be the beginning of a new and more fulfilling career for discouraged and burned-out educators.

Leaving the profession could be the opening to a wonderful and exciting opportunity to use talents and potential never fully developed in the educational field. A noted naturalist and author in our state was once an English teacher who enjoyed bird-watching as a hobby. He left teaching and now leads birding trips for an international organization, conducts local nature trips, and has written a popular field guide as well. Some former teachers have discovered that there is life beyond teaching.

Teachers noting educational trends not to their liking, feeling tired from their positions, or experiencing ill health often opt for early retirement. Individuals so inclined may seek the advice of a financial adviser or local teacher retirement office to obtain information on financial benefits currently available to them. Software is now available that, when given pertinent information such as amount of Social Security, personal investments, and potential retirement date, can help you calculate your monthly retirement income. If it's not enough, you may choose a part-time job to supplement your retirement income. Teacher organizations and state departments of education also offer workshops on retirement preparation.

Many options for constructive change have been presented in this chapter. Some of the suggestions may already be integrated into your life. Others may be new considerations for you. Some may not meet your needs and would be inapplicable in your current situation. For your convenience, all are listed in Figure 2.3. The key shows how you can mark these 30 self-care areas. Those that you wish to consider can be further prioritized in the space available. Once you have isolated your selected work areas, rank them numerically. Beginning with one or two areas, you can start taking charge of your own self-care.

Whether you make simple changes, such as in eating habits or reorganizing your workspace, or more dramatic changes, which may include a leave of absence or even leaving the profession, you can take charge of altering your personal and professional life. Ultimately, you are in charge of your own self-care and the primary beneficiary of the positive choices you make.

Health-Related Habits

- ☐ 1. Diet
- ☐ 2. Water
- ☐ 3. Alcohol
- ☐ 4. Caffeine
- ☐ 5. Tobacco
- ☐ 6. Exercise
- ☐ 7. Fresh air and sunshine
- ☐ 8. Sleep
- ☐ 9. Physical health

Health Enhancers

- ☐ 10. Massage
- ☐ 11. Relaxation exercises

Job Enhancers

- ☐ 12. Time management
- ☐ 13. Efficiency and organization
- ☐ 14. Promptness

Working It Out

- ☐ 15. Self-help literature and tapes
- ☐ 16. Journal writing
- ☐ 17. Growth workshops
- ☐ 18. Self-help groups
- ☐ 19. Professional help

Acting It Out

- ☐ 20. Communication
- ☐ 21. Assertiveness
- ☐ 22. Anger
- ☐ 23. Boundaries
- ☐ 24. Power
- ☐ 25. Goal setting

Making Changes

- ☐ 26. Our physical environment
- ☐ 27. Affecting our work setting
- ☐ 28. Lifestyle
- ☐ 29. Leaving a setting
- ☐ 30. Leaving the profession

Priority Work Areas

- ☐ 1. _____
- ☐ 2. _____
- ☐ 3. _____
- ☐ 4. _____
- ☐ 5. _____
- ☐ 6. _____
- ☐ 7. _____
- ☐ 8. _____
- ☐ 9. _____
- ☐ 10. _____
- ☐ 11. _____
- ☐ 12. _____
- ☐ 13. _____
- ☐ 14. _____
- ☐ 15. _____

Key
A = acceptable level
N = not applicable
W = work areas

Figure 2.3. Self-Care Checklist

3

Building Bridges,
Creating Cooperation

We in education encounter a great deal of stress and are faced with many professional demands. Attempting to deal with them all single-handedly would be overwhelming for one educator because the breadth of challenge is too great. Consequently, it's important to tap the support available from coworkers.

Relational self-care is essential to our well-being and survival in education today and can be created as we build bridges both in educational settings and in outside circles. Support is available formally in organized and structured ways and informally in casual and spontaneous ways (Goldhaber, 1979). It can be obtained from teachers; paraprofessionals; special educators; administrators; and clerical, custodial, and kitchen staff. Support can be exchanged across educational roles and up and down the hierarchy of authority. All of us need it. All of us can give and receive it. All of us can benefit from mutual support. Its existence is a matter of decision, habit, and action, as are all self-care behaviors. When created, support builds on itself and grows within a building and within a system.

Collegial Support

Support among colleagues sometimes comes naturally. Educators who work in supportive climates are fortunate indeed. They are comfortable in their workplace and experience a sense of safety and trust among coworkers and with their administrators. Conversely, those without support experience discomfort, mistrust, and insecurity in the workplace. Where little support exists, suspicion, competition, and divisiveness breed a stress beyond that which normally comes with a job in the field of education.

Much support is already structured and can be used for our professional well-being. The following are examples of formal support.

Teacher Organizations

National, state, and local unions and associations are the primary means of collective and personal support for educators. On a broad scale, they speak out on contemporary issues and defend us against a society that can be critical of our efforts and judgmental of our motives. Union experts guide us in the collective bargaining process, helping to raise our status both economically and professionally.

Such organizations offer personal assistance to educators faced with legal charges. They offer support to employees affected by administrative decisions that they perceive as unfair or with which they disagree. Some years ago, my grandmother was seriously ill, and I thought she might die. According to my contract, I was allotted days to visit a sick parent but not a grandparent. To me, though, she had always functioned as a parent because I lost my dad at an early age. Using this reasoning, a union representative accompanied me to a meeting with our superintendent. Because my grandmother's condition was fragile, she took quick action and persuaded the administrator to be flexible. Union support was meaningful and important to me at a time when I was experiencing fear and anxiety about a personal matter.

Union officers can challenge administration on our behalf when we report perceived unfair treatment. Recently, I spoke at a conference in Alabama and requested a professional day for the meeting. According to district policy, a paid professional day was given only to those who attended conferences in the state of Minnesota. Consequently, I was to lose pay for going to an out-of-state conference. Our union president requested special consideration in my case because I was already paying airfare, meals, and lodging. Again, administration responded with flexibility to current policy and allowed me to take 1 day of "comp" time in order to maintain my present level of pay.

Bringing our concerns to other union or association members and officers is a proven way to receive support and get action on issues that would be difficult or impossible to handle alone. Often, I've fielded complaints by teachers and suggested that they take the concern to their organization. "Oh, no," some reply. "It's not that big of a deal. It's not worth it." Perhaps they are blocked by fear, shyness, or a sense of undeservedness. But to teachers and other educational employees who do make the attempt, it can make a difference in morale, opportunity, and dignity.

Educational organizations also offer opportunities for participation in politics, contract negotiations, and public relations activities through which members can work for the common good. In addition, they sponsor workshops on relevant topics whereby members can gain support from others in similar situations and experiencing similar struggles. Many opportunities are available for group members to exchange woes and be energized and empowered.

Conflict Resolution

District-level programs, such as conflict management training, assist staff in addressing interpersonal issues that arise frequently among peers. In my district, a core of employees from each building is available to provide an objective ear and apply mediative skills to staff conflicts that could otherwise turn into serious misunderstandings. District-level resource persons are also available for staff who wish to consult someone outside their building. I once used such a person and through her help was able to gain objectivity in a building matter that I didn't feel free to discuss on site.

Teams and Departments

Most of us are a part of a work team, whether it be our grade level, department, or crew. Such arrangements can be a natural means of support. Because of proximity, team members provide us with the special understanding of our mutual situation.

A team with which I once taught stands out in my memory as having been particularly supportive. At the time, I took for granted our free flow of conversation about students, parents, and lesson successes and failures. We readily exchanged tips, materials, and laughs. Because we had such a supportive climate, it was fun to stay late, order a pizza, and work on units together. We had not chosen to work together but were formally placed on a team. Not many people have the opportunity to create working teams with others compatible in style and philosophy. Such situations can make our jobs a joy!

Specialty Organizations

Many groupings of educators exist that connect professionals by specialization, whether it be associations of music teachers, counselors, or art teachers. Similarly, there are professional organizations for special educators working in all capacities. For professionals in a unique area of work and who often are the only one or one of few in their building, such groupings offer an affinity and understanding not available anywhere else. I highly value meetings with other EBD teachers, for example, and have attended state- and national-level gatherings periodically just to be around people "who walk my walk and talk my talk." It can be very reinforcing to professional identity and offers opportunity for growth in practice as well.

On the local level, I have experienced cluster meetings organized by a department head for teachers spread throughout the district who operate in the same capacity. Not only are these teachers working with EBD students, but they are also working at the elementary level as I do. To break down our commonality even more specifically, I have met with others who not only teach EBD but also work with another specialization. Beyond what I am able to share with other EBD teachers, we can address the challenge of balancing and separating two and three disability areas. Such positions pose their own unique issues. Thus the more matched our cluster groups, the more we can support one another in dealing with our unique needs.

Mentor-Mentee Relationships

Some school districts provide mentors for new teachers. Such arrangements are excellent opportunities for a starting teacher to process lessons, get relevant feedback, and benefit from a model. New teachers are not the only ones who can benefit from a mentor. Teachers who are changing grade area or field of specialization, or who are fumbling for whatever reason, gain from such support. Mentoring relationships are also beneficial to experienced teachers who are trying to master new teaching strategies called for in school reform literature.

Classes, Workshops, and Graduate Programs

Temporary and long-term formal support can be gleaned from the abundant classes, workshops, and graduate programs available to educators. Participants in such groupings are usually open and willing to share their successes and struggles. Often, teachers will take greater risks with their counterparts in other districts than with those in their own school, team, or district. This freedom is one of the benefits of taking a class or workshop.

Being part of a graduate program often provides a participant with ongoing support because the same people often show up in successive classes, thus affording the opportunity to meld stronger and more enduring relationships. While in graduate school, I benefited greatly from studying for an exam at the home of a classmate or joining a tutorial group for a difficult subject such as statistics. We were all "in the same boat," had the same goals, and were experiencing the same emotions. Because we shared many summer and night classes, we were never at a loss for conversation when it came to discussing our jobs as well as academic pursuits.

On-Site Support Groups

Sometimes, teachers who have an established affinity and similar needs take the opportunity to form their own support group. Together they determine the meeting location and frequency as well as ground rules. Some groups prefer a free flow of conversation and exchange of concerns and ideas. Others establish guidelines to put more routine and order into their meetings. Examples are the following: (a) Each member is encouraged to take a turn checking in and updating group members on professional concerns; (b) an established amount of time is allowed for each member to speak; (c) while each individual is checking in, interruptions or comments are not allowed; (d) time is set aside to discuss individual concerns and give feedback to those requesting it; and (e) an established starting and ending time is consistently adhered to. Each group has different needs and collectively can establish its own norms. What is most important is that participants are heard and given constructive and supportive feedback.

Self-Help and Professionally Run Groups

Although these groups were mentioned in chapter 2, I want to add more in the context of support. Sometimes, educators are placed in settings where a team, an administrator, or the general climate of the building is unhealthy and few opportunities exist for formal or informal support. Teachers in such settings who realize that school is not their "emotional home" often need to process the events of the workplace in a safe and confidential setting. Thus they seek out a self-help group advertised in a newspaper or a professionally guided group provided by a counseling center.

Informal support is available throughout any school district in great abundance. We may already be using it and don't consider such exchange to be support or haven't fully tapped all the resources of this nature available to us.

The Room Next Door

Often, we spontaneously "let off steam" to the nearest coworker if we feel comfortable doing so. Such quick supportive conversations can take place in the hall and on the run. If we need to pop in on a trusted neighbor and briefly share an incident or concern, we may come back laughing at their quip or find we are reoriented by their off-the-cuff wisdom. Our presence may bolster them as well.

Those in close proximity often know our situation well and can rescue us from a variety of potential crises. One year, a teacher I worked with was frequently plagued by a particularly difficult parent. When heading down to the lounge for a break, I passed a teacher leading her class down the hall. She alerted me to the presence of "Mrs. Notorious" in our colleague's room and asked if I could come to the rescue because I was free. When I passed that room, just as I expected, the teacher was getting an earful of unwelcome conversation. Without delay, I popped in and mentioned to her that I wanted to talk. The parent then cut her visit short, much to the relief of the grateful teacher. Because we know each other's situations so well, we can provide this offhand support for one another easily and effectively.

Sharing Space

Often specialists, paraprofessionals, and clerical, custodial, and kitchen staff share common space. Such situations are ideal for spontaneous support. This past year, I shared an office with a team that had a high level of trust. We had an unwritten rule that whatever we unloaded or discussed went no further than "our four walls." Because of the trust level and availability of coworkers, I was able to deal with many issues as they occurred without carrying a load of emotional baggage home. If I got an upsetting call from a parent or experienced an unpleasant encounter with a coworker or student, I was able to process the event and come up with a solution in the presence of a trusted listener. When one of us was facing a difficult meeting or class, we could mention it to another office mate and get "pumped up" and reinforced before we went to the setting. While in the midst of a challenging situation, I was always comforted knowing that I had the good wishes, support, and in some cases even prayers of my office supporters.

Lounge Talk

Support can take on various forms during lunch or a snack break. It's a time to unwind and let off steam with other staff members. Seeking out supportive individuals in these settings is important. None of us needs to endure discussions in which coworkers gossip, complain in a repetitive and negative way, or carry on about personal problems. Instead, it's helpful to spend that time refueling with positive people in whose company is found refreshment, humor, and energy. It's important to plan who you sit by. If you risk sitting by a negative person, it may drag you down for the rest of the day. I've had many great philosophical, practical, intellectual, and humorous conversations in staff lounges by consciously choosing pleasant company.

Another way teachers get support during breaks is through validation of reality. Such questions as "Are your students restless today?" or "Does your class understand the lesson on integers?" can help a discouraged teacher realize that his or her circumstances may be similar to those of others. I find it helpful to test out my perspectives against those of other teachers. One cold winter day, I commented about a student wearing lightweight clothing to school. It concerned me that the child was not properly dressed. When another teacher chimed in, I realized that my thoughts weren't far afield from those of my coworkers.

Outings

An enjoyable and effective way to get support is to go on an outing with a coworker. This could include anything from hiking and fishing to going to a concert or a Chinese restaurant. Another teacher in my district holds a position similar to mine in another school. Together we went to a beauty salon for a manicure and pedicure. While the nail technicians worked on our fingers and feet, we had the opportunity to review our concerns in a relaxed and nurturing atmosphere. On rare occasions, some of us meet at an elegant hotel near school and have a leisurely meal on the terrace. There is no end to the ideas that a few creative teachers can come up with to have support meetings.

Telephone Support

Sometimes, we need to go into depth in discussing an event of the day and do not have the privacy at school to do so. That's when the telephone is an excellent tool for supportive conversation. I have a teacher friend to whom I talk on a regular basis. Our telephone conversations help us process events unaddressed during the school day. I believe we spare our husbands a lot by doing so as well!

A great benefit of telephone support, besides safety and privacy, is perspective. Once away from the school building, one can review an event or discuss a student with more objectivity than when in the actual school setting. Sometimes we tend to view events negatively. While processing an interaction I'd had with a parent, my telephone support person helped me reframe reality by saying, "If a parent had said that to me, I'd have taken it to mean _____ instead of _____." Once we complete a phone session, we're both ready to go back and start fresh and clear the next day.

Built-In Support

Educators who have a spouse, other family member, or room-mate in the field can find support very close at hand. Living with another who works in a similar capacity provides a unique opportunity to experience ongoing daily support. In the relaxed and informal setting of one's own home are people who inherently understand your workplace, professional triumphs, and struggles. They speak your language and know the nature of your concerns. These built-in supporters who work in a school understand when you come home tired, have work to do in the evening, and bring home "emotional carryover" from the school day. You can unwind together at the end of the day or allow the other person time for solitary reflection. One can lend the other an understanding ear in discussions of students who have difficult home situations. A spouse or roommate of this sort can offer perspective if you become too responsible for outcomes over which you have limited influence. They know you well and can detect when you have overworked and should decrease your involvement with a student. Together you can also agree to cut off school-related conversation and move on to another topic more mutually beneficial for the time.

In the early years of my career, I roomed with another teacher. Even though she worked in another school district and taught a different grade level than I did, we exchanged an understanding that cushioned many of the ups and downs of beginning teaching. Our dinner table discussions often included work-related topics such as lessons, parent and coworker challenges, and student needs. We didn't hesitate to share the humorous events that occurred in our classrooms as well. We also learned through trial and error when to put our profession aside, change the subject, or get out for a change of scene. In truth, I don't know if I could have survived without her!

Another opportunity for built-in support is carpooling. Riding to school with a coworker creates a natural situation for engaging in conversations relevant to school and personal concerns as well. Two teachers in my building ride to work together regularly. While driving the freeway to and from school, they not only discuss school-related issues and details of their lessons but also have the opportunity to talk with one another about their families and interests.

"Imaginary Friends"

Although one may have a strong support network and coworkers who are available for continuous support, they are not with us in all educational circumstances. When we are faced with a situation in which we are required to think or act fast, we can turn to what I call an "imaginary friend." To do this, consider what a supporter or composite personality of all our supporters would say if available for discussion right there on the spot. Using the imaginary friend technique is taking the opportunity to realize the skills that we have integrated from being regularly in contact with supporters. The know-how and wherewithal to deal with challenges will come forth from within due to continuous exposure to a support network. We'll know what Jim, Karen, or Pat would say because we benefit from their good sense on a regular basis.

Creating Your Own Network

Perhaps as you've read this section certain individuals have come to mind who make up your support network. Maybe you never before considered them as such. Maybe you are thinking of people you could add to your network. You may be considering someone you could visit after school, invite to breakfast, or call on the telephone just to talk. There might be people in your building with whom you feel a comfort and trust or kindred spirits with whom you'd like to relate more frequently. Maybe you know of another person in your position in another building with whom you'd like to develop a relationship. Could you give that person a call, seek him or her out at a district meeting, or arrange a get-together? I've done that and been straightforward about my motives. More often than not, I've discovered that they had the need to share as well. Observe your setting for a week, alert for possible support. Think it over and then take action. Once we become aware of our needs, surprisingly, we find that assistance is not too far away. Maybe appropriate people have been there all the time, and we just need to take opportunities to cultivate such relationships.

To assist in determining a present and potential network, the diagram shown in Figure 3.1 has been included. Place your name in the center. In the surrounding circles, place names of supportive persons who are already part of your support system. They are arranged according to accessibility with those most immediate in the first circle. Begin by entering the names of those found in your building. The second circle is available for the names of persons in your district from whom you can receive support. This might include others who have jobs similar to yours in other buildings, coordinators located in the central office, or old friends with whom you've taught who are now working in other settings.

Sometimes, it's necessary to make a call during the workday in order to gain support. The telephone spaces represent people you can call for support in or outside your district. If your school has telephones in offices and classrooms, you may find it more convenient to make a quick call to a supporter in another part of your building. Individuals from all three levels can be made immediately accessible through the telephone.

Administrator-Administrator Support

It is common to consider ways that staff can lend one another support, but rarely do we focus on the importance of mutual support among administrators. As staff members, we may see them as persons who should give support, but never consider that they too have professional support needs. To teachers, educational managers can appear to be "in charge" people with everything under control. On closer examination, though, we simply have leaders with feelings and human needs like everyone else. Administrators need self-care or they will be of little use to the staff they need to support! Time and time again, I've heard teachers say that if "they'd give it out at the top maybe it would trickle down to us." Support has to start somewhere— from the school board to the superintendent on down to the principals.

Administrators, however, needn't wait for this magic to come from "on high." Mutual support can begin at any level of educational management. For some, it will mean relinquishing an intense competitive mode. Then, looking sideways, they will discover other administrators on the journey to professional excellence ready to share ideas, even compliments and affirmation.

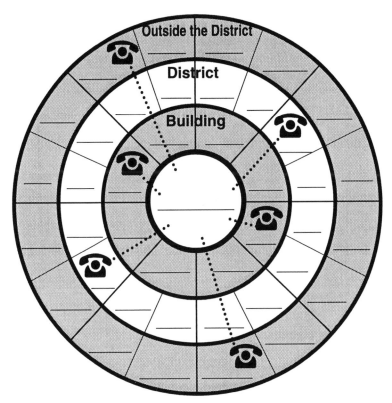

Figure 3.1. My Support Network

It can be helpful for principals to meet for breakfast to exchange ideas. When attending workshops or educational retreats together, they can relate in a casual atmosphere and share firsthand their struggles as well as their ambitions and accomplishments.

This past year, I served on my building management team. One day, while trying to determine the best way to reassign the duties of our office staff, we came to an impasse. Realizing we were stuck, a team member suggested that we ask around the district for ideas. It was so refreshing to hear my principal say, "I'll call over to another building and check with the principal." She knew how to get support and did so automatically. Administrators can contact one another with such questions as "What do you do about lunchroom noise?" "How do you train community volunteers?" or "Do you know where

I could get a good price on a copier?" More than likely, the other party will be not only honored at being asked but more than willing to help.

Communication leads to building bridges, and as these bridges become stronger and more used, support among administrators will increase. It may even trickle down to the rest of the staff!

Administrator-Teacher Support

Administrators are potential key players in any educational employee's support network. As educational leaders, they have the perspective and training to heighten staff awareness of their growth areas and assist them in reaching their professional potential. They are in the position to assist staff with problems and guide them through daily difficulties. From my own experiences and observations, I'd like to list some elements of administrative support that I've found to be most helpful.

Dignity and Cooperation

When I hear of a teacher who has resigned, been terminated, or otherwise left education discouraged and dejected, I can't help but ask myself these questions: "What could an administrator have done to steer that person to success?" "How could this failure have been prevented?" "Where did things break down?" "Was it all the teacher's fault or the administrator's fault?" "Could both parties have collaborated and created a successful working partnership for the benefit of student and teacher as well?"

I recall the time that I was "saved" through appropriate and thoughtful administrative support. During my third year of teaching a self-contained EBD class, my coordinator made the rounds to observe. I thought I was managing reasonably well, considering the student population. He, in fact, said in so many words, "You're not cutting it. Things could be much better." He enumerated my potential growth areas and respectfully suggested bringing in a support team. I was humiliated! My building principal and special education director were immediately informed that a child psychologist and a teacher from a nearby EBD treatment center would be sent to help me.

To help save face with colleagues and maintain my personal and professional dignity, they came under the guise of testing and observing a child. In a short time, I learned a great deal by watching the team interact with my students and in turn trying their techniques. Eventually, I was back on my feet again, more confident and knowledgeable.

Throughout the time that I received support from the center team, I was treated by my three administrators with respect. They continuously looked for ways to affirm me and help me maintain dignity. When I was thanking them at the end of the retraining, one of the administrators told me that they could not have helped all struggling teachers in this manner. He commented that my willingness to "risk the humiliation" and cooperate enabled them to bring me the best resources available. Some teachers, he said, would have continued to struggle alone or given up. To me at the time, it was an offer I could not refuse. I knew no other way to survive professionally. Their respectful approach made me willing to work with them and take the necessary help.

Whenever a teacher is struggling, perhaps deep down that teacher would welcome help. But like me, pride is probably at stake. On the other hand, if the teacher is approached in a manner that will maintain self-respect, much growth can occur for both teacher and administrator.

Many options are available for a principal to help a teacher in trouble. These include providing a mentor or other resource, shifting the teacher to a more appropriate position, and offering personal coaching or constructive feedback. What matters most is the manner in which it's done. Rather than "shuffling incompetency around," an administrator can accomplish more for the greater good by taking hold of the situation, supporting the teachers in their apparent gifts, and providing help and encouragement as they strengthen their weak areas. Constructive criticism, as opposed to threats, put-downs, and intimidation, is far more effective.

Teachers know themselves well. How much better if they would take the offensive in their struggles, approach their administrators as partners, and seek their resources and support to address a growth area. On the part of the staff person, an attitude of openness and willingness to grow is the ingredient needed to make the cooperative effort a move in the right direction. Administrators, in turn, need to provide the teacher with a trusting and supportive atmosphere in which to do so.

Flexibility

Not all staff persons have the same needs. A wise administrator is able to note that and act accordingly.

During a time of strain with a self-contained EBD class, each day for me with these challenging students was getting longer and longer. I expressed this to the principal, although it was probably quite apparent to him as well, and he gave me special consideration. By combining prep and lunch time, I had a full-hour block midday. He agreed to let me work out during that hour at my nearby health club. It was a concession that I greatly appreciated.

Affirmation

All teachers appreciate the boost they receive when given a positive note or comment from an administrator. It makes us feel better and more motivated when our efforts are noticed. Once I returned from winter break and found a note on my desk acknowledging the efforts I'd made since September. Although all staff received such notes, it was still heartening.

Teachers also appreciate spontaneous notice of their quiet efforts to improve the situation in a building. Once I had taken a risk and commented about something at a staff meeting. I was afraid the principal thought I was too bold. Instead, she later remarked that she appreciated my move to get the group thinking in new directions. Had she not affirmed my risk, I may never again have chosen behavior that was new to me.

I once had the privilege of working with an administrator who had a tremendous ability to affirm staff. At the time, I had made a transfer and was quite fearful and insecure as I moved into the new position. In addition, I was coming from a situation where I had received little affirmation and had lost much confidence in my teaching ability. The new administrator was fully aware of my diminished self-concept. Even though I didn't believe in myself, this person believed in my dormant talent and continued to describe to me what

I could become, but did so in the present tense. Eventually, I began to believe the description and gradually my self-concept and job performance reflected that belief. This affirming administrator told staff "who they were" and that's who they eventually became. Administrative belief in me as a teacher and as a person brought me out of a real slump in confidence.

Availability

Primary to the support of staff is the availability of the administrator when needed. Some principals I've worked with have made themselves available by setting up standing weekly or biweekly appointments with their staff. This effectively reduces their anxiety level. Even when staff have serious concerns but can't get in for a meeting immediately, they are always assured of the regularity of a standing appointment.

Another effective means to ensure availability is the appointment of a "backup system." If the principal or director is gone or tied up, a specified person or priority list is made available so that staff know they have support at all times and who they should turn to in a crisis.

Nothing is more encouraging to a teacher than when he or she has the undivided attention of the administrator. I so appreciate my principal saying, "Come on in, Mary. Yes, I do have a minute." Behind closed doors, I am able to get to the heart of my concern in the protected and safe environment spontaneously created to accommodate my need. The confidentiality and respectfulness of such encounters tell staff that their concerns are important and what they have to say has value. The presence and attention of an interested and concerned administrator is optimal support.

Working the System

No one else in the building or department has the power to adjust schedules, influence situations, or make arrangements like an administrator. What matters most to staff is that this is done judiciously and fairly, with the advantage of the staff and students primarily in mind. This presupposes ongoing administrator-staff communication in order to direct the organization most advantageously. A tuned-in

administrator will know how best to route messages, arrange schedules, disseminate resources, create planning and meeting time, and
design the budget in a way that speaks support to all involved.

Adult-Adult Relationships

Those of us who have been in education more than 25 years
probably are witnessing and experiencing as no other staff the tug
and shift involved with redistribution of power. In previous times, it
was the norm to work for an authoritarian administrator who had not
only the final say but in many cases the dominant or only say in
decision making. Thus in such a climate, the dynamics often took on
the characteristics of an adult-child interaction. The administrator in
the adult role directed the organization, and the teacher and other
staff played out the role of child and responded, often following
directions without question. Locked into these roles, educators
learned over time to behave automatically as the dominant or sub-
missive party in work-related interactions. Administrators who
shared responsibilities in their families, took directions from church
and community leaders, and let down their guard on a camping trip
played the role of responsible commander at school. Competent
teachers who ran businesses on the side, directed church choirs, took
charge of their families, and functioned effectively as committee
heads in civic organizations became more docile in their work setting.
Now that the roles are shifting somewhat, the residue of these former
learned behaviors still exists. Some administrators are reluctant to let
go of the tight reins of control and share power, whereas staff are
hesitant to speak out, act assertively, and assume more general responsibility. In other words, both administrators and staff are struggling to achieve adult-adult communication and relational behavior.

There needs to be growth to achieve the mature balance of adult
work relationships. For many of us, this is new territory, as organizations fluctuate toward new structures and models of authority, responsibility, and communication. Old habits sometimes die slowly,
but they can be changed.

Both administrators and staff are beginning to adapt as they
change their thinking and behavior patterns. For administrators, the
challenge is to include staff in decision making and allow them to

participate in areas of management that were never theirs before. For staff, it's the challenge to muster up the courage to step forward and assume their rightful place as participants in building governance. Accompanying this is the abandonment of comfortable mindsets, which in their extremes are, for administrators, "the autonomous boss," and for staff, "the powerless, compliant employee."

How does one throw off a mindset and behaviors that have been habitual and comfortable for so long in order to move into a more adult-adult relational interaction? Can this be achieved by both parties? For administrators, it's important to first and foremost treat staff as adults in every way, calling forth their independence, affirming their abilities to make academic judgments, and eliciting their opinions in the decision-making process. It will require some letting go and at the same time keeping a "steady hand on the throttle." Truly, it requires the ability to strike a balance between old and new behaviors.

On the part of staff, it requires not only standard general courtesy but also abandoning old familiar behaviors. Learning to speak to administrators in an assertive and straightforward manner may take practice, but once it becomes habit both parties know better where they stand on an issue. Some of the old coping behaviors employed by staff to attain benefits for classroom and students can be replaced. Such behaviors as feigned interest in an administrator's family or hobbies, perhaps used to get in his or her good graces, can be replaced by direct, assertive behavior and the negotiating skills of an adult.

In time and with practice, teachers and other personnel who stand up appropriately to their leaders will benefit themselves and their entire setting. As more staff attempt to use and demonstrate adult assertive behavior, their modeling will spread to more reticent staff members and the entire school will become a place where healthy communication is the rule rather than the exception. When adult-adult relationships occur, more authentic cooperation and support can come about.

To further encourage those who find it frightening to speak assertively or even challenge the opinion of an administrator, I'd liked to emphasize that learning a new behavior takes time and it can be frightening. Allowing for the fear and still moving forth at a comfortable pace will eventually lead you to where you are able to speak out automatically and comfortably in an assertive way. In doing so, you will gain the respect not only of peers but of your administrator as well. When you contribute to faculty discussions in a confident and straightforward manner or interact with your principal or director truthfully and respectfully, the principal or director will begin to view you as a competent educational partner instead of an uncertain subordinate.

Not only will the workplace benefit from more honest communication, but you also will find that you can grow in personal power and influence. Ideas that you formerly were too shy or intimidated to express will be not only spoken but also will be put into action. The response you receive for bringing a positive influence into your setting will become a form of support to you.

Another benefit of having adult-adult work relationships is the accomplishment of mutually agreed-on goals. Unless you express your opinion, no peer or administrator can support you and help you bring about your plan. Once I had a serious concern about an issue that I planned to address at a meeting of my special education team. Beforehand, I met with my principal, mentioned my concern, and asked how she felt about the issue. She not only reinforced my thinking but also promised to do so at the group meeting. When administrators know how they can support us, they will. Interestingly enough, in my need for support I was also helping her bring about her agenda.

We interact with on-site administrators consistently. The superintendent and other high-level administrators, even those at the state level, may seem too remote to give us any valuable support. Yet they can be available and worthwhile resources as well.

In my state, special education policy is often in flux, and guidelines for student IEPs change with some frequency. One of my colleagues made it a habit to call the State Department of Education regularly with her questions and asked that their responses be sent to her in writing. She wasn't going over our director's head, but merely ensuring that she had relevant and current information with which to operate. She assertively sought support and benefited professionally from her efforts.

When we write or call a district- or state-level educational official, it's a testament to our own professional caring and concern. If in a state of apathy, one will just go along, remaining at the status quo. When taking a stand and contacting a high-level educational official, an attempt to influence and gain support for personal views is made. In addition, one is reinforcing these beliefs.

Recently, one of my colleagues wrote a very brave and clear letter regarding the effectiveness of a particular curriculum in hopes that a top-level administrator would put support behind a certain educational methodology. The letter she received in response expressed agreement with her ideas, but showed no commitment to action. Still, the writer of the letter gave her opinions and reinforced her own beliefs in the process, and in sharing her letter with coworkers, she gained their affirmation. I, in turn, agreeing with her views, was strengthened in my own philosophy. Thus she achieved modeling, personal reinforcement, and possible district-level influence by seeking support.

Whenever we step out, no matter in how small a manner, we are building our repertoire of communication skills and support-seeking behaviors. Whenever we respond to the needs, questions, and concerns of others, we are building not only bridges for one transaction but bridges that may have broader influence among educators.

Teacher-Administrator Support

Having researched the subject of support, I know full well its value. Time and again, it has been noted as an important measure for prevention of teacher stress. Much has been written about the value of coworker and administrative support. Mentorship and support among administrators has its place in educational literature as well. Nowhere, however, have I seen anything about support given to administrators by teachers and staff!

I have seen, though, national-level educational news articles addressing the difficult challenges present-day administrators are encountering. Educational journals are even addressing the long-known, but little-discussed, lack of support and loneliness school administrators experience. Administrators who have committed suicide and been killed have also gained national coverage.

When I talk about support from staff to administration, I'm not talking about a syrupy or even sincere compliment about a new outfit or snappy necktie. Nor am I suggesting a break of protocol and boundaries to try to become an intimate and confidante. There are, however, circumstances that arise in the natural course of a workday that allow for the opportunity to express what only common courtesy and human decency require.

I recall an instance when a parent, known to leave staff persons on edge, came to school, bypassed the secretary, and angrily burst into the principal's office. This parent literally entered "with a bang" by pounding loudly on the counter. Needless to say, the principal had a difficult session with this individual. Word of the encounter quickly spread among the staff. At the secretary's suggestion, an empathetic staff readily contributed money for flowers for the principal. The principal, of course, was grateful for the well-timed show of appreciation and support. Support need not be given collectively or formally but can be given singularly with a short note or genuine comment. I'm sure many supportive gestures were extended on an individual basis as a result of this incident.

Support can be given in a variety of creative ways. Knowing my principal's sense of humor, I decided to respond to the traumatic incident in a different way. Not having had the opportunity to show my support because I'd been busy most of the day, I took advantage of a break a few hours after the incident occurred and approached the office. I went up to the counter in the main office, replicated the banging noises, then marched around the corner and entered the principal's office. Initially, the shock of again hearing the sounds, which signaled so much distress earlier in the day, startled the principal. However, when I came around the corner, we joined the secretary in a much-needed laugh! Once we all calmed down, the principal and the secretary took the opportunity to tell the story complete with feelings of fear and consternation. For them, it was an opportunity to receive genuine support from a teacher and, for me, an opportunity not only to have some fun but also to get a sincere message across.

Support can come from staff to administration in simpler and quieter ways. It can be in the form of a smile as you pass quickly in the hall, a nod when you agree with something presented at a meeting, or note of appreciation for something said or done that was helpful. Validation, affirmation, gratitude, kindness, and courtesy go both ways and can be given to an administrator by staff as easily and naturally as it can be shared by teachers.

Creating a Supportive Work Environment

Wherever support begins, whether it flows from a teacher, administrator, or other staff member, the important thing is that someone has initiated this dynamic. This initiation of support has the potential to spread throughout the organization for the betterment of all. Positive interchange of support affects an entire team, hall, office, and school building. The school where support is an acceptable and frequently practiced professional behavior contains people willing to grow, try new things, and allow for creativity. It is one of warmth, safety, and caring. Staff members feel free to be who they are as persons and professionals. They experience trust and pleasure in their profession. Such a building sounds ideal, but such characteristics are possible when individuals begin to build the necessary interpersonal bridges to create a supportive climate.

Those who work in education, at whatever level or in whatever capacity, have a natural affinity when they meet in a social setting. When introduced at a party, for example, they have some common understandings to acknowledge. Recently, I met a speech clinician in an exercise class. Even though we were from different school districts and had different jobs, we naturally gravitated toward one another. We had an immediate rapport. While moving about the pool, we discussed our work and the general state of education today.

Regardless of specialization, level of students, or geography, I find this generally to be true among educators. Consequently, I believe this affinity can be used as a bridge builder in the workplace as well as in social settings. Unfortunately, there is the tendency among some of us to "stick to our own kind" in our buildings. Grade areas, subject groups, cooks, special education staff, and paraprofessionals seem to band together and form units. To a degree, such groupings can offer identity and support. On the other hand, they can be exclusionary and divisive. Fear and suspicion come from distance and separatism. Territorial prejudice and departmental exclusivity can detract from the mission of a building. Unity of staff allows for fulfillment of mission and sharing of ideas. Collaboration is far superior to being cliquish when it comes to attaining the purpose of our being together.

Sometimes, the distancing results from lack of understanding, and it becomes a vicious circle. Once groups have the opportunity to understand one another's roles, mutual respect leading to cohesiveness and support can occur. When, for example, there exists misunderstanding between the regular and special education staff, building and department administrators can arrange a special workshop day wherein staff members are given the opportunity to air concerns and discover where mutual misperceptions exist. It can be worthwhile finding out what each group expects and wants from the another. With the new awareness can come the opportunity for better understanding and cooperation.

Closing the gaps between groups is one way to build bridges in a building. There are other means to improve building climate and improve group cohesiveness as well.

Mindsets

How we think about and perceive a situation can sometimes make it true, even if it isn't. We live in the reality we create by the coloration of our perceptions. When we change our perceptions, we can, to some degree, change our reality. For example, if a teacher believes he can gain something from an educator with a different philosophy than his own, chances are that common ground can be established. If an educator believes it's possible to learn from a staff person much younger or older than herself, a good potential for growth exists in the relationship. If a staff person believes he can forge a mutually beneficial communication with another working at a different instructional level or in a different area of specialization, it will very likely happen. In addition, if a school district employee believes she has something to offer or gain from another who is more or less advanced in the system due to pay or position, trust may develop and a bridge of mutual respect and sharing may be built. On the other hand, if staff members are put off by their differences they will remain separated and lose the potential gift of a professional or personal relationship. That's not to discount the probability that there may be certain personalities with whom one has already experienced great difficulties or that one may have a gut feeling that a person would be "toxic" and a relationship ill advised.

Negative mindsets can also be created when one bases his or her expectations about any staff person, whether that person be a principal, cook, teacher, or psychologist, on hearsay or the negative experience of another. Each of us is unique, not only as growing individuals but as participants in a relationship, and each has the opportunity to create a communication unduplicated by any other staff members. Even if our best friend found it difficult working with Mrs. X or had a bad experience at Unpleasant Valley Junior High, we may not necessarily echo her sentiments. All of us live in a different reality and are free to discover and create for ourselves our own perceptions, attitudes, and mindsets.

Manner of Speech

How we approach one another often determines whether we will have a supportive and cooperative interaction or an unproductive and flat interchange. Last spring, a few days before field day, our building phys-ed teacher stopped in my room, sat down, and said, "We'll be outside your window on field day. I just wanted to let you know ahead of time." I was so amazed that someone would extend to me this courtesy that when field day came around, I enjoyed glancing out and watching the various activities throughout the day. Had he not approached in such a manner, I may have seen field day as a distraction and annoyance. Because of his thoughtful gesture, I was enthusiastic about the event and supportive of his efforts.

It's important to consider that everyone is in a different "place" each day. One's disposition may vary due to outside personal circumstances as tragic as family illness or as minor as a traffic tie-up en route to work. If these possibilities are taken into consideration when approaching a coworker or administrator, the chance for a productive and positive exchange is greater.

When working together over time, we know how to read each other and even know what time of day our coworkers are at their best or worst. My body chemistry is such that I experience a low around 3:30 or 4:00 in the afternoon. This was always apparent to a coworker whose desk faced mine in our shared office. My mood was predictably less congenial and slightly irritable at this time. To stabilize my system and mood, I was in the habit of eating an apple at the end of every school day. One day as I sat at my desk grumbling, this teacher, with laughter in her voice, said, "Mary, have you had your apple yet?" She was familiar with my patterns and knew how to read me. Such information about administrators and coworkers will help determine when to best approach someone with important business or even a brief question. When someone is harried, overwhelmed, or irritable, both out of respect for them and on behalf of what you want them to hear, it's best to wait until they too have "had their apple"!

How we respond to one another in the small things makes a difference too. A minor bit of encouragement goes a long way. During my first week in a building where I had been transferred, I was typically anxious about finding things and learning building procedures. I needed duplicates of a paper, but when I turned on the copier, I discovered that it was different from other machines I had used. I fumbled around and bungled the task. A classroom teacher nearby witnessed my struggle. To my surprise, she asked if she could help. My expectation was that she would tease me because I didn't know what I was doing. In other work situations where negative humor was standard fare for some, I had grown to be a bit guarded about my vulnerabilities. When thanking her for the assistance, I explained what kind of reaction I was expecting, and she candidly assured me that I would never be treated that way in this particular setting. She volunteered that her experience at this school had been one of respect and support among teachers. She also added that teachers never bad-mouthed one another there either. I thought I had landed in paradise!

Pass on the Positive

Obviously, negative gossip and irresponsible discussion of the weaknesses and struggles of peers is personally and organizationally destructive. An unkind word can take a nip out of the well-being of another. When information is passed around, it can become distorted and rumors can create unnecessary fears. Conversely, passing on a good word has the opposite effect. Just as the teacher at the copier gave me a sense of safety and comfort in making mistakes, so can taking the opportunity to directly or indirectly "pass on the positive" work wonders among staff.

During a recent visit to my health club, I was walking the track with a group of women. Our conversation turned to their children's experiences in our school district. In the course of the discussion, one talked about the good year her son had experienced and attributed his success to a particular teacher. I was curious and asked who it was. The teacher happened to be someone I worked with several years ago and an old friend as well. I was not surprised that she had taken extra measures on behalf of the child. I felt she should know about what the mother had told me. My first impulse was to go home and call her. Then it occurred to me to call her administrator and share it there first. When I called the school, the principal wasn't in but the secretary took my message. She thanked me profusely for calling and admitted that they rarely heard such comments. I got a kick out of doing it, and I hope I made it possible for three people to experience the positive instead of just one.

Such sharing can be spontaneous or planned. A teacher in our district told me about a class she was taking in which the professor believed strongly in our power to bring positive influence and affirmation into the workplace. As an assignment, the class participants were asked to consider the most negative person in their building. For a predetermined period of time, those attending the class were to regularly compliment and affirm these negative staff persons in small ways. At the end of the project, they were to write up the results, keeping that person anonymous, of course. My friend stated that during the course of this project, she saw "her subject" smile for the first time. As we continued to discuss the experience, we admitted that we often notice many praiseworthy things done by coworkers and even think of many complimentary and genuinely affirming things to say to them but fail to do so. We concluded that maybe we needed to take our thoughts a step further and say them.

As positive behavior and energy spread, they take on power. Those who respond in a negative manner find that their comments are no longer acknowledged and eventually find no social reinforcement for their behaviors. A teacher at a pleasant and positive school once shared that she had been trying to determine what would happen if a negative teacher transferred into her building. She truly believed that one or two difficult teachers could be absorbed successfully there due to the school's lack of reinforcement for negative attitudes. She thought that the newcomers' best sides would come out due to the dominance of a positive work culture.

Staff Inclusion

Much is said about the importance of inclusion of special education students these days. When taken a step further, this concept can apply to staff as well. Inclusion can occur in many forms, such as inviting an itinerant specialist to lunch on workshop day or asking the principal along for an outing.

Frequently, I walk with another staff member after school. Our building recently participated in a citywide contest to motivate employees to exercise. Consequently, our staff became more physically active. On one particular day during the contest, we expanded our usual walking pair to include another teacher and the principal. While leaving the building, we set one ground rule—no school talk. As a result, our conversation was kept lighthearted and off of job-related matters. As four individuals exercising together, we discovered things about our hobbies and interests. Work rapport improved as a result of this inclusive activity.

Consideration has been made in this chapter for the employment of supportive and positive behaviors in the school setting. When there is a mutual exchange of caring, administrators have the freedom to respond with not only their best work performance but also the best aspects of their personalities.

Because a school is composed of living, growing individuals, the relational patterns, interpersonal behaviors, and professional roles may shift, adapt, and modify according to needs and in response to influence. To the degree that staff choose to individually alter their behaviors by initiating support and building bridges, the opportunity to positively influence and transform workplaces exists. In the struggle to break from any old mindsets and negative habits that may exist, a new interdependence can come about. When staff members value not only one another's but also their own contributions, they can create not only a setting that exists for the greater good but also a building in which they themselves can be the beneficiaries of healthy interactions. Many individual staff needs for growth and support can be met in a building climate such as this.

4

Tips for Personal
Intellectual Development

After working in an educational setting all day, we may say, "Intellectual development for me would be just too much on top of everything else!" Some educators, however, have found intellectual development to be a rejuvenating and stimulating antidote for the poison of job stress. The fresh ideas that it provides push out and supplant the repetitive thoughts of the school day.

Like exercise, sleep, or meditative time, an intellectual life can become a healthy part of our daily routine. In planning personal schedules, it can be a worthy substitute for habits that are neither nourishing to the spirit nor meaningful to the mind. In taking charge of our intellectual development, we determine what happens in our own minds instead of forfeiting them to recurring thoughts of the school day.

As educators, we assume the role of leading children along the road of intellectual inquiry. It is rewarding for us to watch students find a topic that greatly interests them and then see that discovery lead to further related subjects as they expand their quest for knowledge. Often, however, we forget that this exciting pursuit can also be an important part of our own lives. We too can have the adventure of learning new things and thus model for our students the joys of learning.

This chapter is based on McGrath (1993).

Obstacles to Intellectual Growth

There are, however, factors in our personal and professional lives that may stand in the way of intellectual development. The following five examples can make the intellectual lives of educators fall short.

1. We have jobs that can drain us not only physically but also mentally and emotionally. When fatigued, it is far easier to assume a passive mode and sit before the television, indiscriminately absorbing whatever it provides. The thought of leaving the house to go out and learn something seems impossible. We believe our tired minds cannot take in one more bit of information, so we shut down for the evening.

2. Family and household demands easily draw us away from our own intellectual centers and scatter us in all directions. When we arrive home after a day's work, we are confronted with the needs of our own children and spouse. Perhaps we must shuttle to a soccer game or the public library. Maybe we have to attend a PTA meeting, this time in the role of parent. Our own children may need assistance with homework. A spouse may want to discuss budgeting, share a situation from his or her job, or ask for help with the snowblower that needs repair. We have groceries to buy, yard work to do, bills to pay, and what about the dusting and vacuuming? Possible diversions from a family and home are endless.

3. "Going to class" is a way of life for educators and in many instances a must for renewing licensure and improving position on the salary scale. It is not unusual to take a class or workshop that looks easy just to fulfill a requirement. Often we sign up for a class with others just to make the experience more palatable. When class selections are made based on reasons other than personal intellectual stimulation, they can create in us a backlash against our own learning.

4. We may be placed with colleagues who, for whatever reason, have set limitations on their own minds, and we take on their attitudes. Sometimes, it is just easier to be like everyone else. If one tries to maintain an interest in personal development while working closely with such individuals, one may

experience subtle pressure to stay back with the group instead of going forth and expanding his or her horizons. "Status quo" educators sometimes resent growing coworkers. It requires some courage to "break with the pack" and enthusiastically pursue personal interests.

5. Often our students' learning needs become paramount, and sadly we neglect our own. Because we are so involved in our particular curriculums, it may not even occur to us to take an interest in a subject beyond those parameters. If learning has nothing to do with our jobs at school, we believe it is irrelevant. "I teach geometry and calculus, why learn Italian?" may be a typical mindset to overcome.

Once we identify these obstacles, they can gradually be addressed and removed. Some impediments to intellectual development are obvious, whereas others are insidious. Consider the five factors and see if any apply to you personally. If so, it may be time to adopt a new way of thinking about your present situation and decide to make changes. In many instances, it is possible to find a new way to grow with little alteration made to your present life.

Ways to Grow Intellectually

Learning can occur whether we're in a relaxed, weary, passive mode or in an energized, more active state. For our purposes, we will define two learning states, passive and active. We'll also address the process of moving from one to the other.

Passive Learning Opportunities

Passive learning is that which influences us and captures our attention without requiring a great deal of output or interaction on our part. While one is in this passive mode, an interest may take hold and lead a learner from passive to active learning. Active learning is that which requires steady engagement and interaction with a task or with other learners. The following are examples of occasions in which educators may open themselves to passive learning opportunities, a description of the process of going from passive to active learning, and examples of active learning situations that may be of interest to educators.

At the end of a workday, we are often tired, and for those times a passive experience is a fitting selection. Thus we can choose from the following intellectual growth options.

Public Radio

Immediately available in the car as we pull out of the school parking lot is the world of public radio. At our fingertips is in-depth news analysis as well as special reports of social, scientific, and historical significance. After being somewhat isolated from the changing events of the "outside" world, a flip to public radio can bring us up to date on what happened during the day. The content of programming leads quickly to a broader perspective of life easily lost during the school day. Some public stations take us down another path and intersperse classical music with news and cultural information. It's refreshing to tune into a symphonic concert and be transported back to the days of Beethoven, Bartók, and Brahms. This learning alternative can elevate the spirit as well as the mind.

Talk Radio

Something is always happening on talk radio. It's generally guaranteed to get the blood flowing and the mind clicking. Such programs, hosted by individuals from both ends of the political spectrum, can spice up the ride to and from work or to another school if we are itinerants. It's interesting to formulate questions and responses as guests express their ideas and listeners call in to share their views. I find it helpful to know what people are thinking on a range of topics. These callers are taxpayers and may even be parents. Their opinions are especially interesting when educational topics are discussed. Talk radio gives us an instant pulse on our community as well as the ready opportunity for intellectual stimulation.

Cassette Tapes

An alternative to car radio and a way to bring life to otherwise "dead time" is cassette tapes. We can access a variety of selected subjects at the flip of a wrist. Books-on-tape are a great diversion. One can look forward all day to the unfolding of a mystery, novel, informational book, or lecture abandoned in the morning when we reached the school parking lot.

A friend working as director of a secondary resource center in a nearby school district is an avid bird-watcher. Frequently, she closes the day by reviewing birdcalls on cassette. With this brief daily intellectual exercise, she is gradually building a repertoire of diverse calls. Her efforts show when she's in the field as she draws on the memory bank acquired through listening to cassette tapes.

Public Libraries

On the way home from school, one can stop by a public library for a brief visit. In the quiet and relaxed atmosphere it provides, one can search for an exciting mystery or a light escape novel or simply sit quietly and read a magazine.

When considering intellectual growth, the obvious choice in reading material is nonfiction. Its expansive content can lead us into the world of gardening, medieval architecture, or tropical fish. Historical fiction is well-liked for both its learning and entertainment value. All fiction offers a variety of writing styles, content, and vocabulary, which can be a challenge to the mind. I once sat next to a man on a plane flight to New Mexico who was engrossed in a mystery for most of the trip. When we visited during dinner, he told me he was a special education teacher from Canada and that he loved mysteries. This teacher went on to share the plot of his book and mentioned how novels and light reading replenished his mind, often weary from school work. Taking our minds on an alternative intellectual track through reading provides intellectual development and also gives it the restful restoration it requires.

If you're not in the mood to read, explore the library collection of videotapes. You may find an alternative to evening television with topics ranging from anthropology to zoology.

Paperback Exchanges

Many communities have paperback book exchanges where for a small fee and a used paperback you can get another one. Often such stores have systems where you can bring in several books and start building up credit. It's fun to browse through their selection, and for a very low price you can sometimes obtain best-sellers soon after they're in regular bookstores. Our school has a paperback exchange located in the staff lounge. It's a way to keep us connected socially and find mental diversion as well.

Newspapers

Many people typically put up their feet and read the newspaper after arriving home from work. Scanning it can provide a quick summary of local, state, and national events. For some, though, the hard-news section may be too heavy, and they prefer the sports or entertainment section. Nevertheless, newspapers serve to move the mind off school and onto the world at large. Any section can provide a basis for discussion. Usually, someone in our lounge is poring over the newspaper during lunch and will interrupt our conversation to say something about the latest ongoing saga provided by the daily print media.

Concerts, Plays, and Cultural Events

While reading the newspaper, you may be drawn to the listing of upcoming local events. Included among these may be concerts, plays, and other cultural events. These are possibilities for restful and passive learning. I often attend our local children's theater, not to endear myself with students or connect with their world in any way, but because I personally enjoy children's literature and find the stories portrayed on stage to be both soothing and fun. I'm intrigued by the antique and modern book editions of the play displayed in the theater showcase and enjoy comparing the illustrations representative of their times. I'm also interested in learning more about the authors and the historical period in which they wrote.

Teachers who buy blocks of concert and play tickets have an opportunity to share intellectual development as they relax together away from school. A group of teachers in my school purchased tickets for an upcoming Broadway show. Attending the production will be both a base of discussion for us as well as a chance to socialize.

Recently, a teacher friend of mine invited me to a Native American worship service at her church. She needed a guitarist for the event, so I agreed to be an active participant in that way. However, by agreeing to help her out, I became a passive learner as I observed the influence of another culture on our worship. While watching the dancing and smelling the incense, I learned a great deal. Unfortunately, I was unable to attend her next church project, a Guatemalan cultural night! Such events require little of us as observers, yet we learn much by attending.

Television

A variety of options are available on television today. Certainly, there is much noisy programming that would not qualify in any way as intellectual in nature. Yet as we tell our students, anything is fodder for an analytical mind. As we sit flipping through channels, we do much discriminatory thinking just by categorizing what we see. On the other hand, quiz and game shows, documentaries, news analysis, and nature programs present the mind with a chance to work and even stretch a bit.

A coworker of mine claims that she learns a lot from talk shows televised during her work hours. Consequently, she tapes them to be viewed when she gets home in the evening. Taping can be helpful for any programming. Much is offered either during the school day or nighttime hours that may be worth consideration for taping.

The programming of public television provides entertainment of a more intellectual nature and also with a quieter tone as well. The fast pace and hype of regular network television is absent as topics from a broad range of solid subject matters unfold on public stations.

Public television's recent series on the Civil War won it great acclaim in many circles. A friend and I missed the original broadcast, so we checked out the entire series from the public library. Over a period of a few months, we got together to enjoy this well-portrayed presentation of a significant period in American history. We often watched the series on school nights. Because all that was required of us was to sit back and receive its content, we were able to grow intellectually even though we were tired.

That particular television series created in me a great interest in the Civil War. It influenced me not only to read books set in that period but also to visit the Gettysburg battlefield the following summer.

Lectures, Travelogues, and Book or Poetry Readings

If we feel passive yet need to get out of the house, a good alternative to staying home might be attending a book or poetry reading at a local bookstore, writers' guild, or university. This past school year, my husband and I attended a series of travel movies narrated live by the filmmaker. It was always a learning experience and relaxing as well.

Such presentations can be meaningful, one-time learning experiences. Our presence at such events enables us to be in a climate where adult growth is encouraged. By attending, we're brought beyond the events of the school day, and again, little is required of us but showing up. Educators may find that attending a function where speaker, filmmaker, author, or poet shares his or her work can be a worthwhile change of pace.

Museums, Zoos, and Exhibits

Observing the pictures and objects of a permanent collection in an art, history, or science museum again requires little effort on our part yet can satisfy and stimulate the intellect. While one is wandering the halls of a museum with no particular focus, anything can catch the eye. Something seen might even come to mind a week, month, or year later as a prompt to pursue the subject further. Maybe something will come up in conversation related to an object viewed in an exhibit and create an opportunity for discussion that would not have been possible otherwise.

Recently, I attended a temporary exhibit of bugs at our zoo. Entomology has never been a topic of particular interest to me. However, I became engrossed in the displays and live exhibits and found myself fascinated as I viewed life forms I had never been aware of before.

Figure 4.1 illustrates the passive nature of the learning just described in the many examples presented. On the arrows, write the ways in which you presently learn passively. In another color, write those you plan to try in the near future.

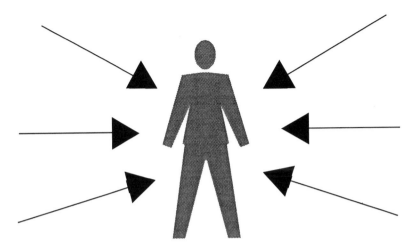

Figure 4.1. Passive Learning Opportunities

Moving From Passive to Active Intellectual Activity

Passive intellectual experiences may in some instances lead to more active ones. This progression can occur immediately or at a later time. Visiting a museum, watching a program on public television, or exposing oneself to cultural activities of any sort can take a learner into new territory as another interest strikes the fancy.

When in the initial stages of recovery from burnout, I was in a passive mode much of the time. I often sat by the window and watched the sparrows come to our feeder. Eventually, I wondered what kind they were and which were male and female. As a result, I looked in a bird guide and began a more active quest for information about these birds. During those months, I often spent time reading through field guides to learn more about birds. It was an incubation period for what I now consider an important hobby. Bird-watching has evolved for me into not only a means of ongoing intellectual development but also a form of relaxation and potent remedy for job stress.

When engaged in a passive learning activity even as seemingly uneventful as reading a novel, watching television, or strolling down the halls of a local history museum, our interest may be captured. Perhaps we'll grab a dictionary or pick up an encyclopedia just to clarify a story event or better understand what really happened during World War I. Whatever the stimulus, a minor response such as that contributes to further learning. It may open pathways of discovery to expand our minds, even create a new interest of lifetime duration. The initial opening to learning may be the energizer of mind, body, and spirit that we need not only to move from the passive to active learning mode but also to bring us beyond the exhaustion caused by our jobs.

Active Learning Opportunities

Active learning, being more participatory and interactive, is often social and offers an individual many opportunities to respond and engage in dialogue with an instructor or other learners. In active learning, one is steadily engaged in the process. It differs from the passive in that learners bring more of themselves into the learning experience. The following are examples.

Institutes and Centers

Foundations and grants sometimes provide unique learning opportunities for educators at little or no cost. The events held at institutes or teacher centers provide opportunities for participants to interact with colleagues and experts in a variety of subject areas. A range of topics is covered by means of panel discussions, field experiences, and individual or cooperative projects. The purpose of such experiences is to renew within educators a personal love of learning, the natural result of which affects their work situation.

They also hold topical sessions that could directly affect performance in the workplace as well. Seminars at a local teacher institute have covered such subjects as architecture in the United States, African American music, environmental ethics, and Native American cultures. Even if these current topics may not necessarily be in one's particular curriculum, they are designed to help educators become broader persons and grow intellectually.

Community Education

Courses offered through community education include such subjects as foreign languages, psychology, and computer literacy. These classes have the advantage of being one-time or short-term sessions for those of us too busy to take on heavy academic work. In addition, they rarely require outside work and so can be taken more for the pleasure of learning than to fulfill a requirement.

Last year, I took a one-session class on how to write a book proposal. Following the suggestions given by the instructor, I wrote several query letters, sent proposals to interested publishers who responded to my letter, and before long found myself involved in this project.

Recently too, my husband and I attended an evening session on travel in Costa Rica presented by a couple who had just visited that country. It was beneficial to meet them and learn firsthand about this Central American nation as we discussed with them their travel experiences.

Our local school district has a community education department offering district employees a discount rate on the class of their choice. My hope is to clear some time this year to take advantage of the opportunity to improve my Italian before I visit relatives in northern Italy next summer.

Home Computers

We needn't go far from home or our own school buildings to receive expert instruction in technology. Apart from taking a formal class in computer literacy, educators often enjoy borrowing or using school computers to expand their skills.

Those who really want to develop their computer expertise take advantage of educator discounts and invest in their own units. Some take them home for the summer or a holiday and use the many tutorial options available for independent learning. The Internet, for example, has emerged as a popular common system for finding information on a variety of topics. This also offers access to consortiums nationwide as well as opportunities for individual educators to communicate on topics of their choice.

Travel

Educators have many advantages over those in other professions because we have more time away from work. This opens us to unlimited travel choices. In any staff lounge across the country after holiday breaks, the conversation turns to where people have traveled and what they saw and did as they share photographs from their latest trips. Looking forward to their next travel adventure is a motivator for educators. Travel refuels the mind with new historic, scientific, political, and sociological information that can't be learned as well any other way. Leisure learning happens incidentally by the very fact that we place ourselves in a different setting. Travel creates interests that can be tapped for a long time to come as it influences reading and other learning choices.

Learning a new language in preparation for and during a trip is an exciting intellectual opportunity. Tapes are available for instruction in foreign languages. Presently, I'm learning Spanish by auto cassette. Little by little, simply by listening to tapes to and from school for 10 or 15 minutes, I'm acquiring a new language. I've found the repetitive and concrete study of language to be an effective and structured way to displace thoughts of my job and its effects. For example, as I'm leaving school thinking, "I'm really tired tonight!" the voice on the Spanish practice tape may ask me to translate "Me gustaría dormir"!

Local Colleges and Universities

Educators can uncover a wealth of learning opportunities at local colleges or universities. Attending classes can be a way of life for many teachers in their efforts to work toward an advanced degree, improve job competence, maintain certification, or improve salary. For some, a college or university is a place to work toward a degree in an area unrelated to one's present teaching assignment. In this manner, individuals attain certification in new areas, making them more well-rounded educators and more employable when layoffs occur as well. I was surprised to learn that one of the elementary school psychologists in my district had once been a high school social studies teacher. My present students were tutored this past summer by a former secondary art teacher who had just received a degree in special education. Another of my special education colleagues added a degree in school psychology to her credentials. Consequently, she was able to broaden the scope of her present job and work part-time as a school psychologist. These individuals made themselves more employable and valuable to their district while they expanded their own knowledge base.

Taking a class in the career area you've always dreamed of pursuing is an interesting way to open intellectual avenues. One of my fantasy careers is that of a news correspondent. I'd love to be in Washington reporting events of international importance as they occur. Because of this interest, I once took a beginning journalism class at the University of Minnesota. Because of the class, I realized the challenges involved in reporting and went more willingly to my job in elementary education!

Embarking on the road to a master's or doctoral degree can be a great adventure in learning. Not only do such programs require an extensive amount of work in a chosen academic field, but along with that often comes the opportunity to select supporting areas of study. During my doctoral program, I was excited to be able to take courses in communications and politics. In fact, being away from the comfortable field of education, I found my ears more attuned to a different type of information. In these classes, I was less likely to tune out the instructor than I would be when presented material in the familiarity of education classes.

Another advantage of higher education is the opportunity to audit classes of interest. Individuals who do so enjoy participating without the burden of writing papers or tests. Teachers whose own children attend colleges find it a benefit to take classes at a discount rate. They may choose to develop themselves in their chosen field, expand their certification, or take something for the simple joy of learning.

Study Groups

Book study groups are especially popular among educators. As an example, the American Association of University Women (AAUW) has several study groups within each local unit. Teachers participating in study groups expose themselves to a variety of ideas in the company of others with a wide range of perspectives. Recently, a teacher at my school injected our lunchroom discussion with details of the life and personality of Eleanor Roosevelt. In doing so, she caught the attention and interest of many. She mentioned that her book club was reading a biography of Mrs. Roosevelt, and from the kind of information she shared, it appeared that her study group went into great depth in their discussions. She appeared enthusiastic about the club and its diverse members. It was apparent that their meeting brought her mental stimulation that she highly valued.

Interest Clubs

Regardless of whatever special interest you might have, there no doubt exists a club composed of like-minded individuals who share it. Clubs are available for those who enjoy hobbies such as birding, astronomy, or photography. Such groups not only meet to share information but also to enjoy field experiences. As a member of our state birding group, I've learned much going on club outings in the company of other nature enthusiasts.

Clubs meeting to develop speaking and writing skills provide growth opportunities for many teachers. Journal writing groups offer members the chance to share personal impressions recorded in their journals, and writers' groups offer critiquing and assistance with writing projects.

Toastmasters International provides its members with the opportunity to develop thinking, listening, and speaking skills in a supportive atmosphere at very little cost. In company with professionals from other fields, teachers in Toastmasters develop their communication and leadership skills in a nonthreatening atmosphere. Toastmasters devotes a segment of each meeting to what is called Table Topics. Members are invited to speak spontaneously in response to a question for up to 2 minutes without prompts or notes. Often the questions are related to the daily news or cultural trends and require quick thinking and basic knowledge of current events. Consequently, members are well motivated to come to a meeting prepared for anything! That means they are attuned to significant events that occur during the week, a natural motivator for intellectual development.

Membership in Toastmasters gives one the opportunity to progress through a basic manual that develops presentation skills. Once this has been completed, members can branch off into diverse manu-

Figure 4.2. Active Learning Opportunities

als dealing with such skills as storytelling, professional speaking, and discussion leading. An elementary teacher who once belonged to my club often entertained us with stories she was preparing for her class. I've used the club as practice ground for speeches and presentations given professionally and received constructive feedback that made the difference in my speaking performance. The skills learned from Toastmasters have also given me confidence to contribute to and even lead staff meetings.

Another advantage of club membership has been the improvement of my grammar. After a presentation, my friends in Toastmasters give me gentle reminders whenever I use familiar speech patterns that are locally acceptable for casual conversation, but not necessarily correct or appropriate in professional situations. I continuously benefit from the company, networking, and modeling of others in the club. As a teacher, I enjoy informally mentoring new members. It's a refreshing change to teach adults who are eager and appreciative of what we as a club can do for them personally and professionally while engaging in our own intellectual development.

To help account for the ways you are involved in active learning, list examples on the steps in the diagram shown in Figure 4.2. Use another color to list new experiences you plan to pursue in this learning mode.

Our Best Learning Opportunity

Association with other individuals who are on a path of intellectual pursuit can be a major contributing factor to one's growth in that area. Conversations with friends or acquaintances in other professional fields can certainly broaden teachers' horizons.

Ultimately, however, I believe that the best resources for intellectual growth that we have are one another. We as teachers are in a profession that gives us ample opportunities for fostering an intellectual life. We are provided with magazines and journals offering us new ways to think about the teaching/learning process.

Workshops are available in abundance to provide professional growth. We are constantly challenged in our field to try new methods and teaching strategies. Some educators choose to take advantage of these options, whereas others do not. The decision to grow is a choice. A choice in the affirmative, in this regard, is one that is replete with many professional as well as personal benefits.

One occasion for exchange potentially conducive to intellectual discussion is our time together in the staff lounge. Beyond our common talk of students and school events lies an opportunity for the sharing of ideas and further pursuing the art of conversation. Intellectual stimulation brings us a dynamism that will contribute to our ability to teach. Exposure to new information can displace the concerns of a workday with fresh ideas and new energy. The positive choice before us is to take charge of our own intellectual lives. Often we can avail ourselves of learning opportunities with little change in our schedules. It may be a matter of making minor changes in how we structure our time. We can, though, create for ourselves what we want for our students: the excitement of having a fulfilling intellectual life. In so doing, the energy created by this growth can contribute to our intellectual as well as emotional survival in the field of education.

5

Attending to the Inner Life: Ways to Grow

The influence of our inner self on both our educational setting and personal lives is hidden yet powerful. Nurturance of our inner life is an important ingredient in the maintenance of physical and mental health and affects our survival in the profession of education. When we nourish our inner person, we have elected to expose ourselves to the life-giving elements that can have enduring and sustaining effects on our whole person for a long time.

The following are eight examples of ways to grow that originate within ourselves. They may seem intangible because they are not always visible to the eye, yet they influence our environment and affect our students, coworkers, and setting in a variety of ways.

Attitude

A prime example of an inner influence on our behavior on the job is attitude. Negativism can become all-pervasive in some workplaces today in the form of unsolicited criticisms that occur during the ordinary interchanges of our daily lives. The very fact that we are exposed to negativism makes us vulnerable to "catching" it ourselves. Our presence in an environment makes us subject to the collective attitudinal poison prevalent in the air in some school settings. It's there for the taking whether we like it or not.

Some negative attitudes are obvious, whereas others are so subtle that their presence is insidious. Around us are people experiencing their own inner tension, anger, frustration, and resentment who show it by subtle and not-so-subtle negative comments. For example, a coworker may make a comparison between your workload and his with a remark such as this: "You have only three students this hour and I have 33!" Along with the statement of fact comes a message of self-pity and an opportunity for the receiver of the comment to feel guilty. Another may say, "This is the lowest-performing class I've ever had!" This for some is an invitation to voice their own complaints about students and perpetuate an unconstructive conversation. Negative comments are examples of wasted energy when individuals, in assessing another's work situation or student ability, are distracted from doing anything to improve their own situation or come up with constructive solutions to help their students.

Cheerleaders for the negative can poison the attitudes of those in their presence, but those in their sphere of influence do have options. The obvious response is to follow the negative person and reinforce their contributions to a staff meeting or lunchroom conversation. One choice is to assume a position of leadership and counter the comments with positive statements. Or one might discourage the negative talk by ignoring it and simply not responding.

Educators who accept the challenge of the last two choices are those who have the strength to encourage coworkers and students. These educators have the self-esteem to maintain their self-selected attitudes and the inner will to uphold a professional and positive work environment for themselves and for others. If faced with a coworker successfully promoting negativism, they choose to respond in a healthy manner. Sometimes this includes removing themselves from a situation. A teacher once told me that the conversations in the staff lounge of her school were consistently negative. The teachers there continuously complained about their students and working conditions and generally framed their circumstances in a negative way. Consequently, she chose to refrain from participating in these discussions and from commenting in similar fashion. Ultimately, she decided that eating alone was her best option. She decided to take charge of her own self-care by creating a lunchtime environment that was more to her personal satisfaction and that contributed to her inner peace and well-being.

Having one's own inner agenda can minimize the times we get drawn into the power of negative conversations and situations that can easily stress and *distress* our inner selves. How easy it can sometimes be to get involved in the agendas of others! To try to prevent this, I've found it helpful to use a children's story in which a small train manages to get up a steep hill by steadily remaining on the track and continuing forward. Keeping a copy of an illustration from the book close at hand has been a reminder to me not to get pulled "off the track" into elements of the job that are not part of my personal agenda. Staying with one's own plans and maintaining one's selected attitude helps to build inner strength and personal well-being in the face of those who would draw you in another direction.

Mindsets affect attitude. How we view our situations can make a difference in how well we function in our own situation and how much we enjoy the job. By this, however, I do not mean viewing the workplace with a Pollyanna-like attitude that denies any challenging realities. I am not in any way recommending that student weaknesses or difficult working conditions be swept under the rug. On the other hand, while keeping a grasp on reality, one can look for the opportunities in these challenges and find means of growth available in such situations. Before one can find opportunity in any potentially dismal situation, it's first necessary to acknowledge the perils and trials there as well.

One weekend, I was particularly discouraged about the type of student we're getting these days. I was focused on those who seemed to be merely existing in fragmented families, needy for attention, and lacking in nurture. At the time, I was on an outing in Wisconsin and in a group with a junior high art teacher. In expressing my concerns, I explained very negatively to her that I didn't think many of these children would be capable of maintaining mature adult relationships because of the many times they'd been rejected, ignored, or abandoned. Her response was an example of attitude as she stated, "I like to believe that these kids will reach for community and find 'family' in other ways." By making that simple statement, she exemplified for me hope and assurance that there's always the possibility that good will emerge for those in even the grimmest home situations. I returned to work the following week with a new courage and hope for the futures of some of my students. I realized that they truly had learned to reach out and bond with many healthy adults such as staff at school who care for them and show it consistently. Certainly, in their need they have been able to seek friends and value relationships in ways that those living in more intact, traditional families will never appreciate. Good things are always happening and are perceived by those equipped to notice. Those able to focus on the positive realities and possibilities existing all around them benefit from an environment created by their own attitudes.

Just as we are capable of seeing possibilities and positives in the lives of our students, so can we access that in our own lives. We may have a passing experience of success or praise that will motivate us to continue in our jobs. The trick is to digest and take in that experience and that truth for sustenance while passing through more negative and discouraging moments. One can grasp positive moments and ride the crest of the motivational wave even though other events that might normally sink us are present. As an example, I save notes from parents, administrators, or staff that are positive and put them into what I call my Kudos File. When I need a lift, I reread some of them. This collection of compliments generally helps restore in me a more positive attitude and sense of personal competence and professional accomplishment.

In a similar vein, when anticipating a challenging encounter with a parent, coworker, or administrator or when one is able to predict a difficult day with a student just by the student's manner on arrival, personal reinforcement is helpful. With a review of positive professional attributes, one can go forth armed with a sense of confidence. With memories of past success and positive professional interactions, one can remain confident in one's ability to handle the next challenge. In spite of any negative exchange that may occur, chances of emerging with self-esteem and personal regard intact remain better for the educator who begins an encounter with full consciousness of his or her own professional competence.

A large component of attitude is gratitude. It could mean the difference between taking for granted coworkers who are always pleasant and helpful, carpeting in our room, baskets that are regularly emptied, or buses that come on time. It seems that we don't realize their value until some minor component of our day goes awry. Only then do we realize the importance of particular people, a small routine, or an expectation. Recently, our buses have been coming late, some as much as a half hour or so. Consequently, the classroom teachers have had to monitor and entertain students in their classrooms after school, which is generally prep time. For them, buses that arrive on time will be very much appreciated in the future and definitely a reason for gratitude.

Gratitude became important to me recently when I read a letter from a special education teacher now on a leave of absence to do missionary work in Africa. She described the bare-bones conditions in the school where she presently teaches and mentioned that a mere notebook for her is now a treasure. She emphasized that she wasn't interested in hearing any complaints whatsoever about our school-related issues! It's all relative, I know, but a tiny shift in attitude with focus on gratitude for the little things could make the day a bit brighter for anyone who chooses to take this slant on reality.

Another way to bolster a positive attitude is what I call the "plug into pleasure" mentality. Thinking ahead about a small treat or anticipating an enjoyable activity planned for the future gears the mind for pleasure and delight. It needn't be something big and could be as simple as looking forward to curling up in the evening with a novel or stopping on the way home for a yogurt cone. This technique can help motivate us through less pleasurable things, such as correcting papers or attending meetings. Although this anticipated experience won't materialize until later in the day, later in the week, or on the weekend, there's no time like the present to begin enjoying it!

Basic to attitude is having an enduring, consistent sense of positive regard and care for yourself. This may not exist in your building or among the administrators, parents, and students with whom you work. In situations in which you receive varying degrees of appreciation, the only person who can sustain, amplify, and, in some unfortunate circumstances, create this is you yourself. We can take care of ourselves either by choosing to keep company with those who will supply us with positive conversation and healthy attitudes or, if little is available externally, by repeatedly giving it to ourselves internally. Striving to maintain a healthy and positive outlook in our workplace affects how we perform and relate in that setting on a daily basis. Ultimately, we are primarily in charge of that attitude.

Affirmations

A way to create or sustain a more positive and affirmative attitude is by applying the technique of affirmations. Because the outer world doesn't always provide positive reinforcement, we must create it for ourselves. Common in recovery and self-help literature, at workshops given for personal growth, and at spiritual retreats is the use of individualized supportive statements known as affirmations. These statements of personal qualities, talent, or accomplishment are repeated to help the individual believe them more strongly. Those who use affirmations may choose to say them daily for a set amount of time in the morning and evening or just once depending on their schedules. Another way people use affirmations is by listing positive statements about themselves in their journals. This can be done either for a set amount of time or by listing a predetermined number of them.

Affirmation exercises are done to overturn a negative trend in thinking or to more deeply implant beliefs about oneself. Examples of affirmations for such reinforcement are included here.

Affirmations Reinforcing Present Reality

- I am a competent teacher who makes a difference in the lives of my students.
- I am a capable social worker and have helped many children and families during my career.
- I am a qualified administrator who makes wise decisions for the betterment of my building.
- I am a knowledgeable media specialist with much technological skill to offer my school.
- I am a talented paraprofessional who plays an essential role in the function of my building.

Sometimes, we get caught in a strong tide of negative thinking and have difficulty focusing on many present positive realities. In that case, affirmations stating desired outcomes can be made. These statements of personal and professional goals are spoken and written in the present tense. Many times we feel uncomfortable saying what we know is far from present reality. It is the belief of those who promote and use affirmations, however, that once we do say affirmations as if they were already a reality that somehow these dreams, goals, or hopes come about. As a result of repeating an affirmation, we may choose behaviors and attitudes that move us in our chosen direction and help us achieve the goals we've developed for ourselves. Affirmations typifying "developing" situations are the following.

Affirmations Stating Desired Outcomes

- I love and enjoy my job and perform it with calmness, confidence, and competence.
- My work situation at _____ School is improving daily.
- I enjoy working with (*insert name of coworker*).
- I am particularly successful working with (*insert name of student*).
- I am comfortable sharing my ideas at staff meetings.
- I have open and positive communication with (*insert name of parent, coworker, or administrator*).

These are simply examples. I encourage you to create your own and watch what happens. With the change in attitude and belief system that comes about from consistent use of affirmations, you may witness subtle or even dramatic changes in situations and relationships occurring gradually over time.

Sometimes I keep my affirmations on the dashboard of the car and recite them during my daily freeway commute. Not only have I strengthened my own sense of worth by repeating to myself what I desire to hear, but I've also witnessed turnabouts in situations that seemed hopeless, after I composed and repeated an affirmation over time. Outer reality often begins in the inner self. Attitudes and situations may take new and surprising directions once they are affected by daily affirmations.

Self-Talk

"You have absolutely no talent!" "You're a terrible teacher!" "That was a lousy lesson!" "You're so disorganized!" If a parent, coworker, student, or administrator made any of these comments to us, we'd be devastated. However, these comments are samples of the kind of self-talk that can pass through an educator's mind daily.

It's amazing sometimes to note the content of the messages we give ourselves in the form of our thoughts. One can listen in on the flow of these thoughts in much the same way we overhear a conversation in the hall outside our classroom. If, during this monitoring of our mind, we "hear" a succession of negative thoughts, we may wish to change the direction those thoughts are taking. Affirmations can be an effective intervention for shifting thoughts into a more positive direction.

"Emergency attitude change affirmations" (Burke, Wilson, & Baker, 1981) can be made to fit any situation that arises. Recently, I was driving to a meeting, somewhat resentful of having to attend outside my regular hours, feeling very tired, and wishing I could be elsewhere. My thoughts perpetuated my attitude. "I don't want to go," "I'm tired and not in the mood for people," and "I can't wait until this is over." That could have been an opportunity for me to inject my mind with some "emergency" affirmations, such as "I will be able to find positive aspects to this meeting," "Being with people is energizing and motivating," and "I will return home satisfied that I had meaningful conversations that will help me help my students." No amount of negative thinking that I was capable of producing in that situation would change the fact that I was required to attend. Why not frame the situation positively and be the beneficiary of a pleasant experience?

We can also distract ourselves from negative self-talk in various ways through conversation, physical exercise, headphones, a project or hobby, or change of scenery. Our minds have to be occupied with something, and it's up to us to determine what that might be. Going out to a hardware store and getting a new part for a lawn mower, taking a quick run down to the nearby pond, or opening up a collection of stamps may be just what's needed to reroute negative thoughts.

Another way to influence negative self-talk is deep breathing. It not only slows the thought process but also calms the anxiety that sometimes accompanies such thoughts. Thus we can break a negative cycle of thinking. Whether we make a mental or physical intervention, we are moving on multiple fronts to change our self-talk to something that builds us up rather than tears us down.

Humor

Another element that feeds or fuels our attitude is the use of humor in all settings in our lives. Presently on the back of my van is a bumper sticker rephrasing an old saying. It reads, "She who laughs, lasts." Because people often turn around to look at me when they pass, I know the message has struck them in some way! Regardless of what they think, when they turn around I'm reminded of the message that I am hoping to give others, the importance of humor in our personal and professional lives. It can come in selected or spontaneous ways. A coworker of mine, for example, chooses to set the tone for the school day by listening en route to work to a disc jockey who hosts a humorous radio program popular with commuters. She swears by his effectiveness in helping her start the day off with a smile.

More and more is being done to inject humor into the lives of educators. Workshops are now available on the use of humor in the classroom. Humor is touted as a means to enhance teachers' relationships with students and influence classroom climate. It is associated with positive peer relationships, creative expression, and the release of tension.

In the "old days," I had a principal who continuously encouraged staff to have at least one good "belly laugh" with their class daily. Coming from him was a wisdom and common sense known among effective educators long before we, with our present-day psychological savvy, discovered it. He knew the importance of humor from having been a successful teacher himself and from observing others who instinctively knew when to use it. He knew the value of humor in bringing a class through a difficult long division lesson or helping them relax. He had probably experienced mistimed cases of the giggles and wanted to avoid unwelcome mischief sure to occur if students weren't allowed the regular release of laughter.

Administrators successfully use humor to introduce routine staff meetings. Often my principal begins by asking who has a joke or story to tell. Often the staff members select from the candid comments of children, a joke they've heard outside school, or funny events that have occurred in their personal lives. The laughter generated succeeds in relaxing us before we address the business at hand.

When anticipating a tense meeting or before presenting a workshop on an unpopular or serious topic, planners and presenters who choose to include humor have the potential to affect positively the climate of the gathering. Last spring, special education staff in our district were strongly encouraged by our director to attend an upcoming fall department workshop on writing IEPs. This is not known to be a pleasant activity or a popular dimension of our jobs. I knew no one who was particularly enthusiastic about attending, but most felt they should go to keep current on the topic and fine-tune their IEP-writing skills. On arriving, we were surprised when our coordinators presented a skit that included a rap music performance complete with costumes. Seeing them looking and acting so out of character put all 100-plus attendees in fits of laughter, which continued to erupt throughout the morning and into the afternoon. When more serious segments of the workshop were presented, participants were more responsive to the subject matter because humor had opened them to the situation. Humor had created a receptivity to content that otherwise would not have been there and appeared to relieve any tension staff may have built up about attending. The day was very successful, and during their preparation our department leaders no doubt experienced a bonding that might not have occurred otherwise. The old custom of starting a meeting with a joke to warm up the audience is a good one. We warmed up to them and to their ideas!

Humor is also successful as a helpful transition. A major transition experienced by those of us in education is the fall return to school. It's traditional in most districts for the superintendent to address the staff in order to review district goals. Generally, it promises to be routine and predictable. Often those in the audience are thinking of all that needs to be done in their classrooms and are somewhat tense and distracted. This year, our superintendent surprised us all. With the help of our district technology department he prepared a video that put us in stitches! The host explained that the superintendent was late for his presentation and that someone had just called his secretary to remind him that all 1,300 Bloomington staff members were awaiting his arrival for the annual address. We were party to the call by means of a prerecorded videotape that showed his secretary receiving the call and reminding him of his missed appointment. The video then depicted a very flustered and panicked superintendent asking his secretary to call the police for an escort. We watched him speeding through town, arriving on the run, straightening his tie, and fumbling with his notes. The video ended and he ran panting and disheveled onto the stage and began his speech to thunderous applause and laughter. By then, as with the IEP workshop, the humor of the introduction created a unified and receptive atmosphere and prepared the audience to hear the more serious presentation to follow. Somehow, humor in which the presenter is the victim of the joke softens the people in the audience to the message and makes them more comfortable. The laughter of an audience is partly saying, "We can identify with your dilemmas and embarrassment because we have had similar flustering experiences!"

Humor can grace days normally comprised of the most mundane and commonplace circumstances. I remember breaking into laughter in the lounge when teachers have reported things said or done by their students and sharing the absurdities of mine with coworkers as well. Fits of giggling are so refreshing. Recently, we had a visit from two animal lovers who brought their pet to school to show the children. This year one of them, with animal in arms, fell asleep during her partner's presentation. Perhaps it was the time of day—after lunch— or the fact that she'd heard him many times before. Nevertheless, she drifted off into a peaceful slumber as she sat stroking the contented animal. Such episodes tickle the funny bone of those who are close to the situation. An occurrence such as this may not seem funny to anyone else, but if you know the people and the circumstances, it's funny, and that humor is often the ingredient that can redirect a serious or routine day into a memorable and joyful time.

Keeping a Journal

An opportunity to nourish, expand, and further one's inner life is available for the low cost of a simple notebook, in which can be recorded experiences, innermost thoughts, and deepest beliefs. This writing can be an opportunity to vent frustrations, release concerns of the day, and work out solutions to problems. The pages of one's journal are open to anything. If one gives oneself permission to freely express everything in a journal, much reorganization, reorientation, and redirection can occur in the inner self.

Journal writing doesn't require great composition skill. In the journal, one needn't worry about spelling, punctuation, or grammar because no one will correct it! It's just a place to use the written word as a vehicle for self-expression, a means of accessing the inner self and arriving at honest emotions and perspectives without being subjected to external judgment or the requirement for sharing the content.

I keep a journal in my desk drawer at school, and if I need to vent emotions, work out a problem, or center myself by reorganization of my thoughts, it helps me to get a better grasp of a situation and arrive at an understanding of myself and others involved. I also keep a journal by my bed. Occasionally, I use it to work out unresolved problems and plan for a new day. Presently, I write in my journal in the morning to get oriented, focused, and geared for the day. It's helpful for me to address any unfinished personal business before going forth into the workday. It's also helpful to dump school concerns there after work in order to assure myself of an evening free of what I've mentally dragged home from school. Generally, the journal is a great outlet for any unfinished emotional business.

Special training for more in-depth journal work is available at retreat houses, personal growth and counseling centers, and community classes. There one can learn specific strategies to better access the inner self, address issues, and target a range of information. I have benefited from such workshops and through books have learned new techniques that help me to be more clear on my personal and professional ideas and concerns. It's sometimes a surprise what can be determined through the inner work done in a journal. It has been a tool to do everything from deciding how to start my day in class to how to reconcile with an alienated coworker, from determining my goals and professional ambitions to releasing resentment and anger so they are not harmful to myself or to others.

Owning a journal, whether it be merely a spiral notebook or a fairly expensive blank book, is representative of the fact that you value your inner life. Recently, a coworker's father died and he expressed to me the next morning at a meeting that during the night, in response to that death, he'd awakened five times and written in his journal. Where else can one express honestly one's thoughts and feelings than in such a special place? Consequently, some of us at work, knowing he valued this mode of inner expression, bought him a cloth-covered blank book. We wanted to acknowledge his form of spirituality and inner relatedness and the process of grief and growth ahead for which the book could be used.

Whether it be for personal of professional purposes, the journal is a fine vehicle for expression of the inner life.

Creativity

Creative expression not only provides release from stress but also gives life back to the tired and weary soul. We in education expend much energy during a workday, and that energy needs to be restored. Engaging in the creative process is an effective means to do so. Whether we take a watercolor or pottery class, turn on the stereo full blast and move around to the familiar strains of old tunes, write songs, or compose poetry, we can access the soul of our being, the inner person, our inner self, our inner child. Whatever we name it, the part of us thrives on creative expression, play, release, letting go and having fun. In our jobs we sometimes lose touch with the part of us that is flexible, that part of us that is free of serious responsibility, our spontaneity. It becomes more familiar to take charge and be structured, programmed, and accountable. Sometimes, if we risk reclaiming or exploring our creative potential and capacity, we can discover some new and exciting parts of ourselves that can contribute to stress management and self-care as well.

Those of us in education often admire creativity when it is used instructionally, but we may not always value it for personal use. If we do come up with a creative art lesson or clever way to present an algorithm, that's one thing. Beyond that, doing it for oneself might be a questionable pursuit for some of us. However, it has value in and of itself, and while engaging in personal creative endeavors, we release parts of our personality that are often held in check during the school day. We are simply honoring our whole being when we allow our inner selves to grow and develop through the creative aspects of ourselves.

If you are unable to access or get a handle on your way to be creative, observe our young people. Children and adolescents seem to come by it quite naturally. Better still, think back on your own youth and remember what creative activities you were drawn to during that period of your life. Did you like to draw, paint, build sand castles, or play with clay? Did you invent new toys, build models, act in plays? Did you like to tinker at a piano or play a violin? If you liked something once and it came naturally and comfortably for you then, it might still be meaningful. On the other hand, maybe you'll find creative expression in a slightly different form. This creative potential, kept under wraps or dormant for many years, is still there and will be readily available again if allowed to surface.

I recently admired a necklace worn by a school psychologist who works in an alternative setting with junior high school students. She responded that she had made it in a silversmithing class she attends at a local junior college. She was excited about her creation and shared that the coral and turquoise used for her projects were purchased in New Mexico. She then showed me the silver ring she'd made as well. By scheduling time for the class, she provided regular time to use her creative capacities and found it to be not only relaxing but personally satisfying as well.

Accommodating the creative instinct allows for relaxation of the mind and spirit. During creative activity, one can rest an active mind with a diversion that nurtures the soul. Sometimes, an idea may come to us during a creative time that is just what we need for a job-related issue. Sometimes, the sole benefit is simply getting away from anything work related and just being.

When we nurture ourselves with creative expression in whatever form, we are able to respond creatively to challenging job situations. Once creativity becomes a more integrated part of us, it also becomes a natural part of our relational and problem-solving skills as we seek solutions to the everyday challenges of the workplace. Creativity applies across the board in self-care, whether it be in devising instructional priorities, managing a difficult student, relating with coworkers who have different work styles than ourselves, or in determining ways to heal the frayed nerves resulting from a hard day at work.

Spirituality

Recently a teacher said to me, "I know we are to honor separation of church and state but actually I pray all day!" So ingrained in us as educators is the importance of this separation that we often forget that all of who we are accompanies us to the job each working day. Our spirituality is reflected in how we relate to peers and students, how we express our subject matter, and how we generally perform as educators. Our spirituality unfolds as we, by the very nature of who we are, express our values and our very being in the school setting.

Spirituality is different for each person and comes about in as many forms as there are educators. Its acknowledgment is important for our development as whole educators and whole human beings. Spirituality for some may express itself in prayer. Others prefer quiet times to listen to their inner voice, the inner stirrings of their heart, whereas others make space in their busy schedules to plan, set goals, write in a journal, or meditate. Each of us accesses and uses our spiritual dimension uniquely.

Because spirituality is different for everyone, it manifests itself on the job in many ways as well. For some, it's the acknowledgment of grace. Those who sense that movement in their lives and see its results occurring claim witness to many small miracles in the lives of young people. As they observe students grasp a small concept or develop in character and maturity, they give credit to the action of grace in human lives. Some experience an assurance of invisible support that may show itself in various forms. Examples are "accidentally" meeting a parent in the hall who is just who they need to see at the time; receiving information at a workshop that perfectly addresses a challenge they're having with a student; or generally sensing an order, meaning, and purpose to the events of the workday. For some educators, spirituality is the sense of confidence that accompanies a life of faith. It is the congruence of having one's beliefs influence actions and attitudes even in the workplace.

For others, spirituality comes in the form of the values they bring to work. Personal morality and the attempt to transmit or inculcate such basic values as honesty, caring, and respect into their students is important to many. Spirituality may take the form of altruism that influences professional motivation. Doing good for others is a strong reinforcement to remain in a job that may not provide a great deal of monetary compensation.

Some educators express their spirituality by valuing the beauty of the present. Building for the future by seizing the moment and resolving to make it count; noticing the sights, smells, and sounds of life; and fully experiencing people and events can be highly spiritual for some. Once, in a teacher newsletter, I saw a photo of a bulletin board that said, "Life is a not a rehearsal but the real thing." Educators who take to heart the concept of living in the present moment notice many small features of life that might otherwise be passed over. They savor experiences that add meaning to the humdrum and routine of life.

From their spirituality, certain educators experience an inner peace and harmony that gives them stability when the outer world is in flux. This stability helps teachers stay grounded when students are continuously transferring in and out of their classrooms due to societal transiency. Stability and grounding gives them perspective on the lives of students and the ability to make sound judgments in the face of daily challenges. It helps them stay calm in the midst of a student quarrel or physical fight. It's part of being clear and organized in the classroom as opposed to being scattered, anxious, and chaotic. Inner peace eases the worry of tomorrow as we trust that events unfold as they should and that we will be equipped to handle whatever comes our way.

Relative to coworkers, spirituality gives educators an extra ability to handle everyday relationships. It allows them to be forgiving of a team member who's offended them rather than carry a grudge. It enables them to apologize when they've offended a student or coworker. Having a self-awareness and self-correction component of spirituality is challenging and difficult at times but accompanies the ability to say you're sorry or to ask for forgiveness when it is fitting to do so. Spirituality enables educators to act with respect for others and to put themselves in another's place. As a result of the understanding gained from this imaginary exchange, they're better able to treat others appropriately as well.

The ability to reflect personally and together with coworkers on the gift of being in education and to express and be in touch with gratitude for our cherished as well as challenging experiences is part of regular growth in the life of some. Spirituality may manifest itself in the ability to gain new growth from adversity rather than becoming bitter. By using a spiritual perspective, some educators are able to see opportunity and gain professional confidence rather than ultimately remain resentful or discouraged as the result of difficult work experiences.

For some, spirituality is seeking prayer support when they need assistance. I have a coworker who is a strong asset in that area, and we exchange concerns to bring to prayer regularly. I have in the past called on a senior friend at my church who has offered to support my work in that way. My communication with her was kept general and confidential. What comes naturally in our personal lives also comes naturally in our professional lives and can be honored accordingly. Our school also has a group of mothers who, with the principal's approval, offered the option to staff to pray for school-related intentions. I chose to take them up on their kind offer and in our communication also keep needs general for confidentiality. Establishing a prayer network has provided me with personal support, and I have been encouraged to see results I believe come from the investment of spiritual work into challenging situations.

Some educators express their prayers individually and privately even in the daily workplace as they bring their simplest needs to a greater Power for assistance. It may seem to them that the small wishes of their heart come into being. As a result of personal prayer, they may be able to turn over a work-related burden; experience guidance in a puzzling situation; or experience a change in attitude toward a difficult coworker, administrator, student, or parent. In company with Divine Assistance, they are able to cope and see positive changes in their work lives.

Another means of spiritual support is the sharing about spirituality with others at work. When coworkers know one another over time, they can become close, and among certain trusted individuals the sharing of the inner journey occurs. I'm part of an informal network of staff interested in health-oriented spirituality, and we frequently share insights and new ideas by passing articles and exchanging books, tapes, and quotes.

For some teachers, spirituality is enhanced by belonging to a faith group for educators. Such groups are sometimes formal and have national roots, whereas others are informal and are created as a result of mutual trust and affinity. Some educators find membership in a religious community or attendance at a place of worship on a regular basis to be a means of steady spiritual nourishment that sustains them through a week of giving, teaching, and modeling for young people.

Other educators are spiritually nourished through nature. For them, the outdoors is where they listen to the stirrings of their heart and renew the spirit. An administrator once shared with me that often after work she let the day go right into a lake near her home as she walked the trail around it. A secondary teacher in my birding group has chosen not to participate in formal, organized religion. Instead, she regularly spends time outdoors bird-watching, and this has become her way of accessing the Creator.

For some, artistic expression enhances and nourishes their spirituality. It may be making a carving, musical composition, or painting of one's own creation, or using the works of others, whether it be meditative viewing of a painting or sculpture or listening to classical music or a Gregorian chant. An observer or listener may not fully understand the meaning of the art he or she encounters but in the deepest self can experience personal sustenance and respond with peace.

To any educator who values spirituality, it is a means to grow and maintain the necessary strength to do the difficult jobs we do. For each, it is different but important. It is a multifaceted part of our inner life and also becomes a part of our career expression.

Solitude

Supporting and closely related to spirituality is solitude. Some of us give and give and give, and we need space and distance and quiet to replenish our energy supply. We need time to fill the "soul holes" created by jobs that can nab sections of the soul bit by bit.

Those who work in the field of education have more time than those in other professions. We are more able to make space for solitude simply by the fact that we have more vacation days and time off from work. We have the opportunity to use this free time to renew the spirit and inner self.

Summer is for me a time to recuperate. I forget that I even work in a school, and other parts of my personality such as wife, daughter, gardener, neighbor, and community member collectively supersede my role as teacher. During summer, the erratic patterns established during the months we are in school are set aside, and there is more time to, for example, establish closer bonds with family and friends, enter the dating scene, get the house clean and organized, have garage sales, do yard work, earn academic credit, and establish regular diet and exercise habits. We're able to take more time for play and outdoor sports such as golf, tennis, or softball. We may be able to fit in some volunteer work, take another job for a change of pace, sit on the deck and read light novels, or travel to distant places. All these activities are fine ways to renew the person. It's only in solitude, however, that we can really get to the center of our being and listen to the heart often drowned out by the ringing of the school bell, blaring of the office intercom, noises of the lunchroom, and voices of demanding students.

When my coworkers return from holiday breaks, especially summer, I notice how refreshed they look. It seems their expressions are more relaxed, their eyes have more sparkle, and they move about the school with more energy. I love being told that I look great, and when I hear that, it's usually during summer breaks after I've had time to rest, renew, and restore my soul. Once school is in full swing, the frequency of that much-appreciated compliment decreases. It is during this time that I look wistfully back on the summer when I've kept a gentler schedule and generally taken better care of myself. Last summer, I had no colds, muscle knots, or headaches! If personal care and refreshment works on a long-term basis, certainly short periods of solitude and restful time apart are beneficial for those of us in the educational field.

Solitude can be for short or long periods of time. It's easier to clear time during extended holidays, but it can be done any time. It can be found in summer while stretching out in a hammock gazing at clouds, in fall while reclining on the sofa watching leaves fall to the ground, in winter while hiding in the cocoon of a tanning booth, or in spring while viewing a flower bed outside the dining room window. One can find solitude by making retreats, renting a hotel room for a night, or even going to a hermitage. The more adventurous can find solitary time camping in the wilderness, hiking an unexplored mountain trail, or traveling through the desert. For each, it is different but it serves the purpose of reclaiming the soul.

Intangible as it seems, the inner life is a powerful part of our existence. It is there at all times whether we are aware of it or not. Our thoughts, feelings, and innermost longings, wishes, dreams, and desires are within us. To whatever degree we choose to acknowledge our inner selves, we are more alive, whole, and vital as human beings and as educators, leading, teaching, and supporting students and other members of the educational community.

A rich interior is prelude to a rich exterior. Nurturing the inner life is a growth option that not only affects our stress and gives us more strength, motivation, spirit, and energy but also propels our whole being further into the fullness of life. It nourishes the self we've chosen to create and sustains the flourishing educators we've chosen to become. Inner growth has a lifelong and far-reaching influence, ranging from the ideals we bring to work to the manner in which we relate to others to how we value and care for ourselves.

6

Creating Flexibility, Openness, and Adaptability

If each of us were asked to paint his or her vision of the educational landscape of the future, say, the year 2020, each would certainly create something unique. No one, not even experts on the future of education, can pinpoint exactly what our jobs will look like in the distant future. No one would be able to give you a survival formula based on an exact description of a future educational scenario. However, no matter what it will be, there are certain personal qualities that will assure our success and ability to survive in this unknown educational territory.

Last year, my husband and I were invited to the home of a friend, a former teacher who is now employed by a local newspaper. Our conversation evolved to a discussion of her job future, and she told us that due to projected technological advances, the present positions of those she supervised would eventually be eliminated. I asked how she planned to address these changes and what she projected for the future of her department. She responded that she had already told her employees that if they remain flexible, open, and adaptable, they could be certain of their career future. Although their tasks would be different, these characteristics would enable them to make changes in the company with confidence. From this conversation, I was given the basis for our survival in the midst of unforeseen educational changes ahead. Just as these characteristics were seen as beneficial by my friend, so I believe the same is relevant for us as we launch into an undefined and uncertain educational future. I'd now like to elaborate on how these characteristics apply to educators.

Flexibility

To survive in the field of education, we will have to learn to live with change and uncertainty. This means we must let go of our comfort level and familiarity with how we've always done things and risk going in new directions, such as moving out of known curricular territory for the unknown of shared interdisciplinary instruction. It could mean letting go of the independent behavior to which we're accustomed and becoming an integral part of a team for instructional planning and shared teaching responsibilities. It could mean letting go of our dependence on the schedules, timetables, and structures that we've always known in exchange for new calendars, starting times, and physical working arrangements. It may mean generating a whole new line of thought in regard to our general approach to educational tasks always done a certain way for so many years. It may mean scrapping lesson plans that have served for 20 years for the unknown of new and different plans. It may mean participating in the development of an evolving curriculum that, like all living organisms, needs re-creation in order to thrive. It could mean sacrificing the certainty of knowing in September exactly what we'll be doing in April for the creativity of following wherever student needs or world events lead. It may mean being willing to board the train and ride into the educational unknown with our competencies and skills ready for use in new ways.

Openness

Moving into educational situations that bombard us with change also calls us to be open to all the pulls and tugs to which we'll be exposed. It does not mean that we abandon our gifts, abilities, training, and assurances of tried-and-true methodologies that work well for students. It does mean, however, that we must be able to balance those against new needs in different settings and in new times. It means asking ourselves these questions: Can what we know work now? Does it fit with the times? What parts of it will have to go? What do I know that will work? Where will I have to adapt and seek retraining? Where will I have to do things differently? Who can help me? How can I do it? What should I surrender? What should I replace? What is my new strategy based on past success but appropriate for this present situation?

To not only ask these questions but also answer them satisfactorily, systems need to allow dream and collaboration time to assure that the creative capacities of educators be used to plan and pioneer new strategies. The bottom line is the ability to come up against the voice inside that says, "This is the way I've always done it," and challenge that voice and say instead, "I have many competencies and job-related skills. Which will work and which must I adapt?"

Adaptability

Once one has loosened the mind and attitude with flexibility and openness, one will be able to move into any unknown situation, setting, work expectation, or challenge with an adaptability that will empower one to succeed. It does not mean hiding in the security of tenure and riding it out to retirement, but being willing to create the vision of our own professional futures. Being adaptable may mean specifically working cooperatively as part of a team, respecting one another's philosophies, differences, styles, and strengths. It could mean coping with downsizing, as is done in business, and being able to assume new roles. For some, it will mean being willing to go through what may seem like constant training to be prepared for whatever is required. Administrators need to consider ways to free their staff for this retooling, such as giving them opportunities to attend conventions, visit other educational sites, and maintain association with educators in their particular disciplines. It may mean moving over to accommodate the talents and offerings of coworkers or being able to step into new paradigms that arise in response to an ever-changing future world. It might mean being a pathfinder, ever willing to work any situation to the optimal advantage of expressed student needs. It may mean surrendering our individual hold on fragmented and territorial work settings for more integrated, whole, and cooperative settings.

To survive creatively, we must be educators who are integrated, whole, and cooperative. We must be professionals who are flexible, open, and adaptable. How can we become this way? By optimal self-care that includes maintaining our physical health and emotional well-being, continuing our personal intellectual development, and nurturing our inner life. If we do this, we can be assured of surviving and even thriving in the ever-changing and exciting educational future we are helping to create.

References

Burke, F., Wilson, D., & Baker, J. (1981, May). *Effective living weekend.* Retreat conducted at the Cenacle, Wayzata, MN.

Citizens Council Mediation Services. (1994). *Mediation training manual.* Minneapolis, MN: Author.

de Mello, A. (1978). *Sadhana: A way to God.* New York: Image.

Freudenberger, H. A. (Ed.). (1980). *Burnout.* Toronto, Ontario: Bantam.

Goldhaber, G. (Ed.). (1979). *Organizational communication.* Dubuque, IA: William C. Brown.

Hendrickson, B. (1979). Teacher burnout: How to recognize it and what to do about it. *Learning, 7f,* 377-379.

Holland, R. P. (1982). Special education burnout. *Educational Horizons, 60*(2), 58-64.

Maslach, C., & Jackson, S. (1981). The measurement of experienced burnout. *Journal of Occupational Behavior, 2,* 99-113.

McGrath, M. Z. (1993). *Teachers! Do you (develop your) mind?* (Pamphlet available from Phantasia Press, 104 Woodcrest Drive, Burnsville, MN 55337)

Monsein, M. (Speaker). (1978). *Breathing and relaxation* (Cassette recording). Minneapolis, MN: Monsein Clinic.

Owen, L. (1994, June 8). Lower fat is the higher standard in school lunch. *Saint Paul Pioneer Press,* pp. 1A, 6A.

Progoff, I. (1983). *Intensive journal workshop.* (Available from Dialogue House Associates, Inc., 80 E. Eleventh Street, New York, NY 10003)

Relaxation skills take-home tape (Cassette recording). (1974). New York: Core Communications in Health.

Selye, H. (1976). *The stress of life*. New York: McGraw-Hill.

U.S. Department of Agriculture. (1992). *The food guide pyramid* (Home and Garden Bulletin No. 252). Hyattsville, MD: Human Nutrition Information Service.

**CORWIN
PRESS**

The Corwin Press logo—a raven striding across an open book— represents the happy union of courage and learning. We are a professional-level publisher of books and journals for K–12 educators, and we are committed to creating and providing resources that embody these qualities. Corwin's motto is "Success for All Learners."